LESS STRESS BUSINESS

*A Guide for Hiring, Coaching, and
Leading Great Employees*

JAMIE SUSSEL TURNER M.ED

ISBN-10: 0615985335
ISBN-13: 9780615985336

Library of Congress Control Number: 2014904863
Less Stress Publishing
Sea Bright, New Jersey

Dedication

To my mother, Sonia Sussel, and father, Allan Sussel,
for their love and encouragement.

Author's Note

The content of this book expands and amplifies what I have written in my blog at LessStressBusiness.com. I have altered details and names for all unidentified anecdotes and quotations and edited quoted notes and emails for brevity and clarity.

As a school principal, I enjoyed exposure to many ideas and opportunities. Some I felt prepared for; others required more learning and created more stress. Still, I felt a responsibility to students, parents, staff, and the school board to meet whatever challenges arose on any given day.

When I made a career change in 2009 and became a coach, I saw how well the stresses of my career in education worked in preparing me for supporting the growth of business owners. I share that understanding with you, and I hope you keep this book handy so you can refer to it when stresses arise in your work and personal life.

Contents

Acknowledgments

The lyrics to Alanis Morissette's anthem, *You Learn*, deeply resonate with me.

> *"You live you learn. You love you learn.*
> *You cry you learn. You lose you learn.*
> *You bleed you learn. You scream you learn."*

I'd like to take liberty with Morissette's lyrics with the addition of the following line that reflects my intention for this book,

"You live you learn. You learn you teach."

I have been a teacher since my sisters and I played school in the basement of our childhood home. I have also been fortunate to have amazing teachers in my life—and I'm not only talking about the ones I encountered in a classroom. I'm talking about those special people whose paths have crossed mine. Those people who have been patient with me, angry with me, frustrated with me, understanding of me, loving of me, and provided me with so many lessons. I deeply thank the special people from whom I have learned so very much.

- My clients who have so graciously opened their hearts and minds to learning—with special thanks to the following clients for the extra time they gave in interviews for this book: Connie Aliverto, Lisa Aquino, Richard Bach, Rob Bixon, Mike Martorella, Marta Mehlmann, Jen Neumayer, Marilyn Schlossbach, Marty Thompson, and Christine Zilinski;

- The students, teachers, administrators, and parents in the Fair Haven [NJ] School community who allowed me to grow my leadership skills among their halls, classrooms, and lives;

- My colleagues at NJ EXpedited Certification for Educational Leadership (NJ EXCEL) and the aspiring school leaders who attended my classes, listened to my leadership lessons, and have gone on to create their own;

- The leaders of The Teachers College Reading and Writing Project, especially Lucy Calkins and Shanna Schwartz, for sparking and edifying my journey as a writer;

- My first leadership coach, Diana Williams, my extraordinary leadership trainer, Dennis Sparks, and my coaching colleagues from International Coach Federation of New Jersey (ICF-NJ) for helping to launch me as a coach, especially Lynn Schaeber, Andrea Harvey, Rob Imperato, Erica Loren, Marijo Puleo, and Claude Blanc;

- My coaching colleague and author Michele Lederman for connecting me with my amazing writing coach Henry DeVries, who was instrumental in the vision and direction for this book, as well as many of the catchy chapter titles;

- Susan Scott, Deli Moussavi-Bock, Aimee Windmiller-Wood, and the entire team at Fierce, Inc. for my deep and lasting journey in having and teaching fierce conversations about building a better world;

- Laura Belsten and her team at The Institute for Social + Emotional Intelligence for deepening my knowledge and application of this critical field, adding true benefit to my development as well as to the growth of my clients;

- The best book club ever: Erika Casriel, Mary Beth DiPrima, Mary Fleck, Paula Freed, Barbara Johnson, Antonia Martinez, and Gail Pfeifer for teaching me to read with a new mind and new eyes;

- My special professional friends who became my closest personal friends— The "Skirts": Julie Botel, Janie Edmonds, Susan King, Claire and Jerry Kohn, and Mary Fleck for our shared leadership adventure, deep friendship, love, and lessons;

- My dear friends Nancy Aufiero, Elizabeth DeGiulio, Pat Dippold, Carol Epstein, Gene Freed, Marianne and Art Greenwald, Sue Gronback, Diane Hampton, Vivienne Kellem, Lisa Luckett, Tery Michaud, Kathy Mulleavey, Lisa Neri, Nancy Saltzman, Caryn Berman, Ginny Kamin, Sheila Ravin, Janet Roman, Rachel Weitzenkorn and Helen Zax, who heard more about my blog and book than they probably cared to—and still cheered me on;

- My developmental editor extraordinaire and treasured friend Gail Pfeifer for her brilliant organizational mind and for pushing me to dig deeper and be more clear on every single page of this book;

- My gifted copy editor Sharron Stockhausen for making my words and meaning flow properly;

- My creative graphic artist Joni McPherson for her brilliant design for my cover and promotional materials;

- All my Turner relatives, San; Barry; Linda; Brent; Sue; Glenn; Matt; Sarah; Meredith; Colin; Jo; Shaun; Kate; Paul; Jenny; Heather; Scott; Brad; and the best little granddaughters ever, Jillian and Amy; for, even with my late arrival, making me feel like one of the family;

- My inspiring and brilliant sisters, Laura Lurie and her husband, Glenn, and Andrea Sussel and her partner, Larry, for their devotion, compassion, wisdom, unconditional love, and understanding, and my loving nephews, Daniel, Jacob, and Toby;

- My son Josh Horowitz and his girlfriend, Jessie Wasserman, and my son Adam Horowitz and his wife, Arame Ngom, for their loving support and many fierce conversations;

- And mostly to my incredible husband, Wayne Turner, for supporting me through every step of this project by being my "ghost thinker," master proofreader, personal chef, and the love of my life.

How My Story and My Stress Can Lead to Your Success

Leadership is influence.

—John C. Maxwell
Author, Trainer, Leadership Expert

My business as a leadership and communication coach is built on the shoulders of a thirty-seven-year career in education, which taught me much of what I bring to my current career. I was first a teacher, then a supervisor, and spent the final twelve years as an elementary school principal. While difficult issues could arise with individual students and pressure from parents, I found my most significant stresses came from the day-to-day leadership of people. Those early days of leading a school of 450 students and seventy-five staff members both energized and challenged me. While it was exciting to see how each day would unfold, many situations arose for which I had no reservoir of experience. Some teachers resisted change, some had conflicts with one another, others gossiped about me, several wanted to maintain the status quo, disagreed with my decisions, or perhaps just didn't like me.

It would have been great to leave all that at work, but those problems followed me home, consumed my thoughts, and worried me outside the job.

Leading the staff meant learning, over a period of time, how to hire and retain the right people, how to give and garner feedback, and how to consider the value of varying points of view. The broad range of beliefs, values, and personalities often made it hard to create an atmosphere that would accomplish our mission, which was to provide an excellent education for our children. Our school community had to find better ways of building and maintaining our relationships with each other—especially when many of us saw things differently—in order to achieve that goal.

I struggled to influence others and realized that if I couldn't figure out how to do so in a positive way, I couldn't call myself an effective leader. More times than I can count, this realization required me to grow leadership muscles that had been weak or non-existent. I had to learn how to say yes to less stress, which required me to:

- listen better so I could hear varying points of view,

- stop focusing on only *where* the staff needed to grow and shift my perspective toward looking at *what* they were already doing well,

- muster the courage to confront underperforming employees and team dysfunction,

- cultivate clarity, grace, and skill when having difficult conversations,

- delegate deliberately and with follow-through,

- stop taking things personally, and

- adhere to my values while understanding when and how to be open to feedback so the viewpoints of others could influence me as much as I influenced them.

Knowing I couldn't accomplish all of this on my own, I sought out leadership coaching, inspirational books, pertinent workshops, and more experienced colleagues. I learned what it took to hire, coach, and lead through lots of trial and even more error. Gradually I experienced more good days than bad. Some of my best days were when a teacher would have an "aha" moment, and I could see her growth right before my eyes.

As I made strides in my leadership skills, I could feel the stress melt away. And as I felt less stress, I was able to lead with a calmer presence, fewer debilitating emotions, greater clarity, and better communication. This resulted in more trusting work relationships and allowed me to have a more balanced and relaxed personal life. I can help you develop these skills, too.

If you take home job stress from dealing with challenging employees, if this stress keeps you from focusing on the big picture and leaves little energy for the growth of your business, if you want to lead your staff with less stress for yourself, then this book is for you. I'll share the lessons I have learned and, if you apply the less stress business practices I developed, these lessons will guide you toward success by improving your communication and management skills and uncovering how you can lead your business with less stress than you ever imagined.

ONE

Say Yes to Less Stress: Practice One

We can only control our mindset—how we see things. We can't control things beyond our control, but we can control our response to what happens. There are very smart high level executives who get swallowed up by situations outside their sphere of control.

—Mike Martorella
Executive Coach and Former CEO

Can you remember the last time you felt completely relaxed and not worried about your business? Probably not. The challenge of leading people—far more than any other factor—is often the main source of stress for managers, leaders, and business owners like you. And improving employee performance is always at the top of my clients' agendas, just as it is at the top of yours.

It is possible to manage your business *and* lead your team with less stress than you ever imagined. I've seen it done, and I'm confident that if you say yes to less stress, you can achieve this goal, too.

The Seven Less Stress Business Practices

In the chapters that follow, you will discover seven practical and easy-to-use tips—my Less Stress Business Practices—that I've developed and distilled from the thousands of hours I worked coaching and training leaders. These practices grew out of the key changes and discoveries that transformed the businesses and lives of my clients—while also significantly reducing their stress. When I asked clients to rate their stress at the start of coaching on a ten-point scale, with ten being off the charts stress, every client was at nine or higher. After implementing the practices in this book, they each reduced their stress to two or three. For most clients that signified a 75 percent reduction of stress! By acknowledging and addressing what was contributing to their stress, my clients learned how to reduce it.

The Less Stress Business Practices are also designed to shift your viewpoint and help you see how your own thinking and behaviors might be contributing to the stress you are feeling. Applying these practices will enable you to take charge of your growth in a way that will alter how you take charge of the growth of your employees. This will reduce your stress so you can devote more energy to taking your business to new heights—and have more of a balanced life at the same time.

Implementing new behaviors and changing your thinking will require practice, perseverance, patience, and continued use. As the expression, "the Queen Mary doesn't turn on a dime," illustrates, you will need to maintain steady and consistent attention over time to keep yourself, your team, and your business heading in the right direction. I recommend you read through all the practices in the book first, but as you read, consider which issues in your business are causing you the greatest stress. Those issues will give you an idea about which business practice you might decide to implement first. These practices are designed so you can implement them in any order along the way. There's no one formula for success. Each of my clients traveled a unique journey in reducing stress, working one new practice at a time based on specific personal and business needs.

Here are the seven practices that will get you where you want to go:

1. Say Yes to Less Stress
2. Aspire Higher When You Hire
3. Keep Talking When the Honeymoon is Over
4. Open the Door to Feedback
5. Ready, Aim, Fire That Employee!
6. Delegate or Die Trying
7. Confront Dysfunction so Your Team Can Function

First, let's clarify the typical types of stress encountered by business owners and managers. I'm sure these will sound familiar since it's natural to feel stress as you go through your daily life. Some of this stress is good. For example, when you suddenly think, *Yikes, I've got to pay the phone bill,* your heart rate might increase or you might begin to breathe more rapidly. That's *normal* stress and is simply your body becoming energized to prepare you for action. This kind of stress can jump-start you to complete tasks and overcome obstacles.

Chronic stress is another matter entirely. This is the kind of stress that keeps you on edge, disrupts your sleep, and creeps into your personal life. For example, you may ruminate about the financial viability of your business. This worry might find its way into your thoughts every day. You may get lost in the maze of available options and possibilities or maybe you've put your head in the sand, afraid to face your business situation, whatever that situation is.

When you separate your chronic stress into two categories—the things you can control and the things you can't control—you can begin to refocus your energy toward what you can control.

To keep from getting swallowed up by spending energy and resources on things beyond your control, you need to shift your perspective toward expending your mental energy and activity on what you can control. This is the first step toward saying yes to less stress.

On the other hand, chronic stress can come from two places: (1) focusing on what you cannot control or (2) avoiding taking positive action when possible. Some researchers report that chronic stress can lead to depression, illness, and even biological aging. According to *The Harvard Business Review,*

> *The American Institute of Stress reports, roughly 60 percent of doctor visits stem from stress-related complaints and illnesses: In total, American businesses lose $300 billion annually to lowered productivity, absenteeism, healthcare, and related costs stemming from stress.*[1]

The same impact is true for relationship stresses. In the workplace, these stresses may show up as interpersonal conflict or as holding on to feelings that seem too frightening to express. For example, you may know you should have a conversation with a certain employee about performance, but you end up having that conversation only in your head. As one of my clients said, "Some days, I've taken stress from a conflict at work home with me and lived with it for a whole weekend."

As a business owner or manager, you've experienced a healthy dose of good stress and it's likely that it helped get you to where you are. Maybe you're a hair salon owner who is a master stylist, a restaurant owner who got your start as a breakout chef, or a top-producing real estate broker. Regardless of your business discipline, you know what it takes to excel and you generated the track record to prove it.

When getting a business off the ground, optimism runs high—no one starts out saying, "I think I'll dive into a losing business." So you hire the best employees you can find, design and equip your ideal location, launch your marketing plan, and wait for your business to take off. But the responsibilities of launching a business, as wonderful as that may seem, carry a lot of daily stress you may not have anticipated. It doesn't take long before you start to feel the weight of decision-making, finances, long hours, and personnel problems. This stress is even more pronounced if you're a solopreneur and face these types of pressures alone. If you have a partner, there is the added complication of maintaining a solid working relationship with your partner as you struggle to share leadership. All of this stress can accumulate and take its toll on you, showing up as back pain, chronic headaches, angry outbursts, sleepless nights, impatience, or no time for a personal life. You might get frequent colds, find yourself tightly gripping the steering wheel on the way to work or on your drive home, or notice that your breathing becomes shallow.

Nearly as soon as the stress of the start-up phase subsides, you get hit with new challenges from all directions. Your manager becomes pregnant, the economy tanks, and healthcare costs rise. You quickly learn leadership will take its toll on you—if you let it.

Here's a short and true story of mine that explores how certain assumptions may fuel stress.

— It's Not a Tug of War —

One summer, after participating in a camp horse show, the counselor asked me to take the horse I had been riding and put him into the trailer for the trip back to camp. All of about twelve years of age and never having done this before, I replied, "Sure," without thinking through the situation.

I stood facing the horse, holding one end of a rough rope attached to the horse's halter. I took tiny steps, backing up onto the trailer ramp. But the more I pulled the horse along, the more he resisted. I began to yank at the rope with an encouraging, "Come on now. Let's go." But the horse's nostrils flared, he swung his head in the air, reversed direction, and stomped away, ripping the rope through my hands. For what felt like hours, I sat with my rope-burned, pain-stricken hands in a bucket of cold water wondering, *What's wrong with that horse?*

I learned much later that the proper way to lead a horse into a trailer is to walk beside him and slowly step up the ramp, without looking back, acting completely confident that the horse will comply.

My horse-trailer moment became a powerful metaphor for how business owners sometimes hire, coach, and lead employees. That day, it never occurred to me that either my method or my lack of knowledge about how to do the task, which I had never done before, contributed to creating the problem. I assumed I knew what it took to trailer a horse; I simply didn't know what I didn't know. But the whole experience taught me two valuable lessons:

1. Going *against* someone with force achieves little more than pain and stress.
2. Going *with* someone in a shared direction leads to accomplishment and shared success.

In the same way I thought I had a stubborn, uncooperative horse, many business owners begin their roles as managers and leaders completely frustrated by employees they view as stubborn or uncooperative. Owners think something's wrong with the employees and wonder why they don't just do their jobs the way the owners expect them to.

But hiring, coaching, and leading employees is not a tug of war. If you experience it that way, with yourself tugging at one end of a rope and your employees resisting at the other end, the scene is set for one big power struggle. If you fear conflict when telling your employees your expectations for their performance, your stress will escalate. You'll walk on eggshells and everyone in your workplace will feel the tension as well. Here's how one of my clients, Jen Neumayer, the owner of a European Wax Center franchise, describes her experience:

> *In my early years, I tended to internalize stress and never accurately communicated with my associates. So instead of nipping the problem early on, I would hold it in and not say anything, due to feeling pressure that I needed that employee. Eventually I would wind up exploding when the tension finally became too much. If I had talked with the employee about their behavior*

*early on, we could have had a much more amicable relation-
ship – instead of internalizing it or expecting them to read my
mind.*

Maybe this is where you are right now. Or maybe you are pretty good at
managing most of your team but you deal with a few employees who push
your buttons and you don't know why or what you can do about it.

Take a moment to imagine having employees who show initiative, stick
with projects, follow procedures, have a positive attitude, meet expectations,
offer suggestions for a better way, and are a significant force in making your
business successful and your life less stressful. Can't you feel the stress lifting
just by imagining this possibility?

As my career transitioned from teaching to leading to coaching leaders
of many different businesses, it became crystal clear to me that the skills we
need to excel in our chosen fields are very different from the skills we need
to help others excel. When we're good at what we do, we often harbor a blind
spot when it comes to getting employees to do it too. We might make assumptions and neglect to go back to the beginning steps that got us to where we are.
Perhaps we forget what it was like to not know how to do something, much as
I did not know, nor was I told, how to lead my horse into that trailer.

Yet it is possible to stop the tug of war and lead our employees in a shared
direction. When we find new ways to hire, coach, and lead, we experience the
added benefit of reducing our stress. It takes commitment, passion, and a willingness to look within—a willingness to grow. And when we take *ourselves* on
in this way, we learn to create the conditions in our workplaces that can result
in the employees and business of our dreams. We can say yes to less stress.

Keep reading and I'll show you the way.

TWO

Aspire Higher When You Hire: Practice Two

If you hire people just because they can do a job, they'll work for your money. But if you hire people who believe what you believe, they'll work for you with blood and sweat and tears.

—Simon Sinek
Author, Optimist, and Speaker

Employees are your number one asset, your number one liability, and can be your number one source of stress. They can make the difference between a thriving business and an unevenly delivered customer or client experience. This chapter will explore simple strategies you can use to begin to build the team of your dreams. It all starts with hiring like it matters—because it does.

As Jim Collins, author of *Good to Great: Why Some Companies Make the Leap...and Others Don't*, writes,

> *The executives who ignited the transformations from good to great did not first figure out where to drive the bus and then get people to take it there. No, they first got the right people on the bus (and the wrong people off the bus) and then figured out where to drive it.*[1]

When you aspire higher when you hire, you not only reduce your stress but you also create a foundation for your team and for your business's success. I live at the Jersey Shore, where Hurricane Sandy devastated our small town of Sea Bright in October 2012. Buildings all over town suffered crumbling foundations because of this catastrophic storm. Most had no remedy but demolition. Months later it was not easy to watch bulldozers lop off sections of homes and businesses and then dump them into disposal trucks. Barren blocks remained where life and commerce once flourished.

I've noticed something similar can happen to the foundation of a business. Problems (like storms) appear that cause the substance of the organization to crumble. When you don't aspire higher when you hire employees, you limit the possibilities for building a solid foundational team. When you don't hire like it matters, your business won't be able to withstand the storms that inevitably occur—storms such as the first wave of distrust, difficulty, or dysfunction will topple your people—your foundation—and add to your stress.

The key to building a great foundation lies in having high aspirations when you hire employees. This requires planning, clarity, and a lot of preparation. But many business owners respond to the pressure of needing someone to fill a vacant position by simply rushing to check the hiring task off their to-do list; they neglect to clarify the qualifications of the job and check references, and they may conduct interviews that are too brief. Instead, they nab the first person who barely meets a list of somewhat fuzzy qualifications. To make matters worse, business owners repeat this haphazard process until they end up with an employee who kind of fits the bill. To aspire higher when hiring and find the employees who are the best fit for your business, take a closer look at the following specific strategies used in Practice Two.

Smart Hiring Starts with Clarity and Interview Preparation

Successful hiring starts well before the interview begins. It is crucial to take time to prepare before the candidate even walks through the door. Here are the strategies and specific steps I use to coach business managers through the interview preparation process:

- **Get clear about what you value.** Ask yourself: *What personality attributes and character traits will be the best fit for the business and our team?* This will help you get a picture of the kind of person you want to hire.

Remember, you're hiring a human being whose values will add to or detract from your mission.

- **Get clear about the skills needed.** Make a list of the skill set that would be the best fit for the position. It's likely you won't find someone who has all of the skills you need, so tease out which ones are essential and which ones you can teach.

- **Get input from others in your organization.** How would the interviewee's future coworkers describe their ideal team member? What do they feel is needed to create a balanced team? What qualities do they think are needed for the job? When you include the candidate's future coworkers in the process, it empowers them to contribute to the new employee's success.

- **Generate questions.** Start with a consistent base of questions you will ask of all candidates. This allows you to compare responses to the same questions. Then be fully present and listen deeply to the interviewee so you can probe to learn more based on the answer given. Expanding on the questions will help you dig deeper and uncover more about the applicant based on information he or she provided to your basic question(s).

- **Pre-screen applicants.** Have the person who schedules the interviews begin to gather a sense of the candidates during a brief phone interview. Generate a list of qualities the scheduling person might observe such as manners, response time to scheduling the interview, communication skills, energy level, enthusiasm, and any questions the applicant might ask. Take time to hear and value the scheduler's feedback.

- **Consider the interview setting.** Do you want to be seated at a table? Behind your desk? Meet over a meal? Do you want to conduct the interview alone or include other team members in the process? Determine the mood and atmosphere that would be most conducive to providing you the best information about the candidate, then plan for that. I have always conducted interviews with at least one other colleague present. While the other interviewer was asking a question, I was better able to take in all sources of information such as body language, eye contact, and tone of voice, allowing me to observe and listen more fully.

Most of the steps are concrete ways to prepare for an interview, except for the first step, which addresses values. But value clarification can be one of the most important ways you find your best-fit employees. Here's an example I use with my clients.

> I once interviewed a teacher who cried at her interview. The tears welled up when she identified kindness as one of her best attributes. I followed up by asking, "What made you value kindness?" She quietly dabbed at her eyes as she talked about lessons from her mother, who had recently passed away.
>
> Years later, she told me that she left our meeting thinking, "I'm sure I blew that interview! There's no way they're hiring a teacher who cries."
>
> But that was not the case. As the door closed behind her, my colleague and I beamed at one another, "She's just what we're looking for!"

How did we know? We knew we were aiming to hire a teacher who was not only smart, but one who had heart as well. These were values we admired and saw as essential for the wholehearted and nurturing teacher who would contribute to a thriving classroom and also to a positive school community.

Seeing emotion bubble up during the interview was evidence of her *heart*. How she responded to our other questions was evidence of her *smart*.

Crying during an interview wouldn't have the same outcome in all businesses or for all positions. In some scenarios, a crying candidate might land immediately on the do-not-call-back list. What's the difference? It's all about aspiring higher by fitting the hire with what you value. As my client, chef/restaurateur Marilyn Schlossbach learned from our coaching sessions,

> *Our work with core values has really put into perspective that we deserve the best people that fit us. Before we always thought we were never going to find people as good as us. Opening ourselves up in conversation to understanding who we really are, and making those conversations part of our hiring process, have made me believe there are people out there that can help us.*

Time spent at the front end of the interview will reduce stress and save time in the long run by avoiding the need to go through the hiring process again if a hastily chosen candidate doesn't work out. From investing time in the interviewing process, one of my clients expressed the positive impact on her growth this way:

> *I've gotten to a point where I can be picky. I'd rather be short-staffed than hire someone I'm not 100 percent sure of. I now have a loyal staff who understands the impact of bad hiring and will pitch in until we find the right person.*

So maybe you believe there's no crying at interviews or you might see crying as a positive sign. Either way, when you know what you're looking for, you can measure each candidate against your criteria and have your best shot at figuring out who will be the best fit. And by the way, that crying job candidate turned out to be one of my best hiring decisions!

Design Interview Questions to Uncover APCs (Attitude, Personality, and Character)

The skills people bring to a job vary and people's job skills grow over time. But attitude, personality, and character—what I call the APCs—are not likely to change. So, just as you learned your ABCs are critical to reading and writing, you can learn how focusing on your APCs will be the essential element of hiring the right person for your business. This process involves being able to uncover these essential qualities in a candidate because if you hire someone with the right skill set but the wrong APCs, you will pay a steep price in a variety of ways. One price can show up as a drama-filled workplace when a new employee turns out to have a me-only attitude that wreaks havoc with the teamwork culture you've worked hard to build. Or you may pay a different price when you discover a new hire lacks integrity when he or she says something will get done, but it doesn't, and the inaction gets covered up with lies or stories.

Questions to help you uncover a candidate's APCs

As a school principal, I interviewed thousands of candidates for various teaching and support positions, and one of my favorite questions designed to evaluate a prospective teacher's APCs was, "So, what have you read lately?"

Many applicants would hesitate to answer this question. For some the hesitation was due to a lack of educational reading and they mentally scrambled to find something that would suffice. Others responded with a questioning tone, as if to ask, "Is that what you want to hear?"

These were the three most typical replies:

1. Gee, I don't know.
2. Let's see. I think I read an article about, uh, math?
3. I'm almost embarrassed to say. But, you know, it's summer, and I love to read steamy fiction at the beach.

Which of the above replies do you think was the best fit for what I was looking for? It was choice number three. That's because I placed a high value on authenticity and honesty—as well as on reading. I wanted to know if the candidate was a reader and if that person could give an honest answer, even if it meant admitting potentially embarrassing reading tastes. Of course, candidates seemed even more appealing when, in addition to being honest, they could name and discuss an influential article or book about education.

When you ask a question and see the candidate's eyes glance upward and to the left or right, when there's a pause, when the candidate takes a deep breath, you know you've hit the interview question jackpot. You've likely landed on a question that will really get the candidate to think on his or her feet. This is most likely to happen when you ask open-ended and atypical questions—the type of question that causes a candidate to be thrown from the typical well-rehearsed response. When you find that question, listen intently and you'll notice the candidate's all-important APCs begin to emerge.

Here are more sample open-ended questions and what each one might help you uncover:

- **In your last job, what made it a good day?**

  Look for:

  - Do they demonstrate a positive attitude? Are they focused on others (versus self) and the impact of what they do on others or on the organization? You might follow up with, "So, what made it a bad day?"

- **What are you passionate about?**

  Look for:

  - Do they have an energetic attitude or one they think you expect? Do they light up? Is their passion something that fits well with what you're hiring them to do? Are they just giving you the answer they think you want?

- **What does your clothes closet look like?**

Look for:

  - Does their personality show strength in organizational skills? If so, they will describe a closet with like items or colors together. Maybe you'd prefer someone with a more random personality. In that case, look for a closet that is not so highly organized. There's not a right answer here—look for what would be your best fit.

- **What are you most proud of?**

Look for:

  - Do they mention character traits like perseverance, honesty, kindness, or self-control? Do they focus on material possessions? Do they highlight relationships or family? Again there is no right answer here. Be sure you know which traits you most value.

- **How do you handle conflict?**

Look for:

  - What is their conflict attitude? Do they see differences as an opportunity for growth or something to be avoided at all costs? Try to tease out their behavior to see if they hold grudges, take revenge, and/or use passive-aggressive tactics? Follow up by asking for an example of a time they had difficulty confronting a coworker, how they handled it and what they learned from the experience.

- **What do you do when you don't know what to do?**

  Look for:

  - What is their personality around collaboration? Do they see others as part of their team? Do they have initiative? Are they resourceful? Do they know when to ask for help? Do they dive into research and never come up for air? Do they investigate policies, consider culture and regulations? Or do they figure things out on their own?

- **Describe a situation where things didn't go well or you failed.**

  Look for:

  - What kind of failure do they share and what is their demeanor when they share it? Is it something of significant impact to them? Are they willing to show you their warts? How do they handle failure? What is their attitude about challenge? Do they see failure as a learning opportunity?

Spotting and Developing Leadership

Sometimes you might be so focused on posting positions and interviewing external candidates that you overlook talent right under your nose. So, how can you spot leadership potential in your current employees? And how do you know a future leader when you see one?

Whether you want a romantic partner or new couch, it helps to know what you're looking for. The same is true for spotting leaders. When you have a great working definition of what a leader looks like, it's easier to find one.

There's no shortage of leadership definitions. In her book, *Daring Greatly: How the Courage to Be Vulnerable Transforms the Way We Live, Love, Parent, and Lead* researcher and thought leader Brené Brown offers one that seems to tap into something others don't. Brown writes:

> *My definition of a leader is anyone who holds her—or himself—accountable for finding potential in people and processes.*[2]

Here are the five traits of potential leaders on which I place the highest value.

1. **Vulnerability:** Leaders aren't afraid of being seen, being known, and being wrong. They don't shy away from difficult conversations or thorny issues. They offer feedback generously, including positive feedback, expressions of gratitude, and opportunities for growth. In a word, leaders aren't afraid of being vulnerable.

2. **Learning:** Leaders are lifelong learners. They read voraciously, attend professional conferences, reflect on their beliefs and actions, and share what they learn willingly. They continue learning even if they have to pay for it themselves.

3. **Initiative:** Executive coach and former CEO Mike Martorella spots a leader when the person says, "I'd like to take a shot at this." So, look for future leaders who offer ideas and action without being asked or prodded. Future leaders don't complain about the way things are—they engage others in finding a better way. They often watch your leadership very closely and take initiative in discussing with you the choices you make and what's behind them. They are often students of leadership without even realizing it. As Sheryl Sandberg writes in *Lean In: Women, Work, and the Will to*

Lead, "It is hard to visualize someone as a leader if she is always waiting to be told what to do."[3]

4. **Responsibility:** Leaders accept responsibility when things go wrong—without placing blame on others. They own their part in whatever happens and they mine failures for learning opportunities.

5. **Teamwork:** Leaders have passion for helping others to become their best. Leaders know they can't go it alone. They focus on "we" and "us" more than "I" and "me."

Spotting a leader is step one. Step two is launching that leader. For example, I was a twenty-four-year-old teacher when my principal Dr. Mary Lee Fitzgerald asked me, "Have you considered going to graduate school?" At the time, graduate school was the furthest thing from my mind. I was getting ready to leave teaching to become a mother, with no plans to ever return. But she didn't let up on me and even wrote in my evaluation that year, "Jamie has a great deal to contribute to the teaching profession and, perhaps, public education in general." I enrolled in graduate school the next year, which led to a thirty-seven-year career in education, the final nineteen as a curriculum supervisor and principal.

I was launched by Dr. Fitzgerald, who had a vision for my future that wasn't even on my radar screen. What can you do to launch the leaders in your midst? Have you told them what you see ahead for them? Have you written about their potential so they can hold on to your vision? It's been more than three decades since my mentor did that for me, and I have enormous gratitude for the impact her words and confidence have had on the leader I have become.

Step three is keeping your mind and intuition primed for spotting leadership examples in your daily life. My first flight on Southwest Airlines in the spring of 2012 brought me face-to-face with the results of exceptional leadership that resulted from great hiring. Here's what happened.

"Hooray, we're taking off—and we have brakes that work," squealed the Southwest flight attendant after a frustrating ninety-minute delay. "We're as happy about it as you are," she added with a laugh.

Despite the frustrations at the start of my return flight from Phoenix, it turned out to be one of my happiest flying experiences ever. What made that so? The flight attendant's attitude played a key role by setting a fun, upbeat, human tone, which helped me put frustration aside and adopt a these-things-will-happen attitude.

This was my first Southwest Airlines experience, so I was surprised to hear a refreshing take on the typical rehearsed scripts as the flight attendant delivered the safety information without the mechanical phrases I usually just tune out anyway. I found myself tuning in instead and even saw two flight attendants hugging as the plane's door was sealed shut, clearly ecstatic to be finally taking off and comfortable showing it. Other airlines might label this as unprofessional behavior, but to me, it was refreshingly real.

"I'm so impressed with your positive vibe and how real you are in speaking to the passengers," I told the flight attendant mid-flight. She beamed in reply, "Well, that's because Southwest hires for attitude."

I was curious to learn more about how they did this, so I asked the eighteen-year Southwest veteran to share a few of Southwest's interview questions and how they uncover an applicant's attitude. Here's one example she gave: "Have you ever had a conflict with a coworker?" Figuring most folks would have encountered some turbulence in their workplace relationships, she said that the interviewers look for how candidates resolved the difficulty. An answer of "No, I always get along with everyone," would imply they may avoid conflict and not be willing to work at having solid coworker relationships. This implication would see to it that the candidate didn't make it to the next round. And Southwest has many rounds, each one requiring 100 percent agreement of the interview team.

In *Lessons in Loyalty*, one of many great books about Southwest Airlines, the author and former Southwest employee Lorraine Grubbs-West summarizes their hiring this way:

> *At Southwest Airlines, people are hired for their attitude and trained for the skills they'll need to do their jobs. Money is seldom a motivator. In fact, many—like me—actually take a cut in pay to work there!*[4]

Southwest knows how to uncover APCs and has clear corporate values that are conveyed by their employees because Southwest aspires higher when they hire. Their employees' positive attitudes rippled down to me, and I could feel the difference as a consumer of Southwest's services.

Take some time to look around you and notice signs of leadership. Leaders exhibit a variety of personalities, so be careful not to miss the quietest member of your team. Be careful not to miss the employee who is very different from you. The most dynamic teams are made up of people who offer (or possess) different skills and different personality traits. When you think you've found a leader, watch that person more closely. Delegate a project and see what happens. The promising leader will show you potential—just be sure you're on the lookout and don't miss the leader under your nose.

And, don't forget to notice those candidates who exhibit a great sense of humor. A friend relayed that one of her favorite funny interview moments occurred when she asked, "How would you deal with an unhappy client?" Without missing a beat, the candidate replied with a smile, "A swift kick to the knees," before answering for real. My friend added, "Her sense of humor was what got her hired, and she became one of our best employees, even though she had less experience than other applicants."

Interviewing is not an exact science—there's a "gut call" factor involved. So, keep your radar tuned in, your manure meter turned up, and probe when your "gut alert" goes off. Designing open-ended questions that uncover a candidate's APCs and leadership abilities can help you find someone who is the best fit for the values and beliefs you want your business to represent.

THREE

Keep Talking When The Honeymoon is Over: Practice Three

Each conversation we have with our coworkers, customers, significant others, and children either enhances those relationships, flatlines them, or takes them down.

—Susan Scott
Author of *Fierce Conversations*

Hiring an employee is not the end of the process for launching new employees—it's the beginning. If you want a Less Stress Business, how you develop your relationships with your new employees is key to how successful they become.

Imagine a new romantic relationship. In the early stages, the couple's conversation leads to deep discovery about each other's likes, dislikes, and personality. They're getting to know one another and it's an exciting time; however, this early stage, typically called the honeymoon, doesn't last forever. After some time, the couple enters a new phase—let's call it reality—and things start to feel different. Some of that early excitement has diminished. They don't reveal all of their warts at the start of their union so inevitably they hit a few bumps in the relationship road when they encounter challenges with the other person that trigger emotional reactions. These difficulties and conflicts cause them to begin to see each other's true selves for the first time. How the relationship unfolds during the reality stage has a lot to do with how the couple communicates. When they keep talking to each other after the honeymoon is over, they increase their chances for a happy, lasting, relationship.

Much the same happens in the business relationships you have with your employees.

This chapter will give you some key skills for enhancing relationships by implementing Practice Three: Keep Talking When the Honeymoon is Over. The first step is to take a closer look at some typical patterns of behavior between you and your employees that may make having conversations with employees difficult for you.

Starting the Conversation

Once the honeymoon phase is over, you begin to get to know the people you hired as complex human beings with stresses of their own, rather than as just good hires. Perhaps instead of having the all-star team you envisioned, you have some employees who routinely disappoint you, which can amplify your own stress level rather than reduce it. Maybe you spend countless hours wondering how to turn your underperforming employees into high performing team members by asking yourself what they need from you. When you ask this powerful question you will find that some may need motivation. Others may need incentives. Still others may benefit from ongoing feedback and simple acknowledgment that they are on the right track and you value their efforts. You may discover the lazy employees you thought you had really just needed more support than you have provided. You can learn to approach these floundering team members even when you feel uneasy at the thought of venturing into a confrontation. Having these conversations will become the cornerstone of your employee on-boarding process and also help you to decide whether an employee is the right fit for your business (more about this in chapter five).

Over the years my coaching clients have vented to me about employees who begin to show up differently than they expect. It can be intimidating to think about confronting employees, but you can learn the skills needed to deal with these issues and begin the important work of keeping the conversation going. Here's how one client, Christine Zilinski, industry leader and owner of Salon Concrete in Red Bank, New Jersey, expressed her growth in confronting her staff and how doing so helped improve their performance, which also led to a decrease in her stress:

> *I used to let things build up. It's like I wouldn't empty the garbage can of conversations I needed to have at the end of each day. I'd even be in the shower talking to myself and then never end up having the conversations. Now I feel like I'm emptying the garbage can, and I'm able to have conversations in a calmer, less emotional way.*

By learning how to address employee issues when a problematic pattern first emerged, rather than waiting until the problem escalated, Christine learned how to have calmer conversations. These conversations enhanced her relationships with her employees and improved their performance. She increased her business by 30 percent and relocated to a better location with triple the space, all while reducing her stress rather than adding to it.

One way to accomplishing this kind of Less Stress Business lies in identifying problem behaviors that may emerge after an employee has been hired and settled in.

EGGSaggerated Workplace Moods and How to Crack Them

A bad mood is one of the first signs that a new employee may have kept some things hidden during the hiring process. A moody employee creates a pothole in your road to success that can turn into a sinkhole if it's not quickly addressed. Everyone has a bad day now and again, but it is how one handles those days that is important. When an employee routinely inflicts bad moods on everyone around, others are left asking, "What did I do to deserve *that*?" The concept of considering emotional intelligence in business offers business owners insight on why people's moods impact performance. In the book *Primal Leadership: Realizing the Power of Emotional Intelligence* the authors, Goleman, Boyatzis, and McKee, made the case for businesses to not ignore the power of our emotions. The authors say:

Negative emotions—especially chronic anger, anxiety, or a sense of futility—powerfully disrupt work, hijacking attention from the task at hand.[1]

It may take just one employee with a consistently negative mood to bring everyone down, impacting productivity, teamwork, and customer service. Moods are contagious, and no one likes catching someone else's bad mood. I've created a model of what I call EGGSaggerated workplace moods. Look over the examples and determine if any of them are polluting your workplace, causing everyone to walk on eggshells. See if any match how your employees (or maybe even you) show up at work.

- **The Scrambled Egg:** Manner is mixed up, confused, and unfocused.

- **The Omelet:** Appears to mix with others, but actually remains closed and distant in both mood and emotion.

- **The Over Easy:** Eager to please and be liked; allows others to take advantage of them and falls apart with any pressure.

- **The Deviled Egg:** Attractive at first glance, but uses devilish ways, such as manipulation and undermining, to get what they want.

- **The Hard Boiled:** Inflexible, determined in their thinking, and set in their way of behavior.

- **The Eggs Benedict:** Above it all, conceited, too important to do menial jobs others are required to do.

If one of these descriptions matches one of your employees, that's a sure sign it's time for a meaningful conversation. You might be hesitant to confront an employee about mood either because mood isn't actually part of the job description or because you are uncomfortable with confrontation. But the longer you allow the problem employee to carry on, the more damage that person will do to your workplace culture. Even worse, a negative mood may filter to your customers and turn some away. So you need to find a way to confront an employee with a troublesome mood so you can clearly set an expectation for having "Sunny Side Up" employees.

I have found two communication tools to be helpful in confrontational conversations. The first is called The Five Words. This tool provides a template that builds upon five easy-to-remember words and helps you clearly and succinctly outline the problem from your point of view. The five words for this template are: When you...I feel...because. Psychologists often refer to this approach as an "I" statement. Here's an example that shows how you can confront an employee with an "Eggs Benedict" mood that is reflected by inattention to a job responsibility:

> **When you** leave at the end of your shift without sweeping the floor, **I feel** confused and frustrated **because** this is a job we've discussed and something each assistant is responsible for.

Once you've delivered your five-word statement in a neutral and calm tone, be prepared to listen for the employee's response. Often the employee will defend his or her actions or blame someone else for the problem. When that happens, remain calm, use a soft tone, and simply add,

> Thank you for helping me to understand the complications from yesterday. I want to be sure you understand your responsibility is to do this every day from now on without any reminders.

When there is no change following a five-word conversation and an employee's mood continues to infect your workplace, a more in-depth confrontation conversation may be needed. Here's a sample conversation I crafted with one of my clients.

Cindy, I want to talk with you about the effect your mood is having on our restaurant team. Lately there have been times when you seem to be in a bad mood. For example, yesterday you slammed the door and stormed to the kitchen without saying hello to anyone, and last week you sat with your arms folded and head down at our shift meeting. I feel upset for our team and concerned for you. This is important because everyone's mood impacts the overall tone and feeling of the restaurant and our ability to create a great experience for our guests. It's also important because I'm concerned you may have something weighing you down. I may not have made it clear to you how important it is to show up with positivity each and every day. I sincerely want to work with you to help you resolve the issue of how your mood impacts how you show up to our team and guests. I would like to hear your thoughts on this and I'm ready to listen.

When you take time and care to confront an employee whose mood and resulting behavior is impacting the workplace, it will help create the culture you want. On the other hand, stress escalates if you just grit your teeth and fume inside when an employee has a pattern of behavior that passes a bad mood along to others. If you value a happy and productive workplace, then it's up to you to have the conversations that let your employees know how you feel and what changes are expected. Here's how one of my clients, Lisa Aquino, owner of Brahma Yoga Spa, expressed her learning in this area:

Whatever the dynamic of each employee relationship, there is something I am doing or not doing that is allowing the relationship to exist. I have to dissect our interactions from my perspective to see what I can do to achieve a positive connection with my employee. I can't change the other person, but I can change myself by speaking up and managing the employee more effectively.

One-on-ones can be a great technique for allowing these kinds of conversations to happen. Read on to learn how.

One-on-Ones: The Bridge that Moves Employees from Mediocre to Magnificent

Bad moods aren't the only topics that need leaders who are skilled at and willing to initiate a conversation. What's talked about in your business is what gets attention. Consistent, powerful, and authentic one-on-ones are the places where you can have the biggest influence on your team and the places where they can influence you.

Here's one of the most frequent complaints from my coaching clients: "Why don't my employees change? I've told them the same thing a thousand times and nothing is different." My clients usually raise this question when they're ready to pull out their hair with frustration at an employee's lack of growth. They often label the employee as lazy, unmotivated, or a bad fit. While that could be true, it also might be true that the client or the manager just hasn't found the right approach to lead the employee to success, developed skill in having conversations that lead to growth, or simply carved out the time to contribute to the employee's growth.

So, when was the last time you sat down with your employees individually and really asked, really listened, really cared, and really helped them to grow? If your answer is, "More than a few months ago," then you're like most leaders I know. You haven't yet discovered the simple power of the one-on-one.

Each time I coach leaders who commit to making one-on-ones a consistent part of their leadership practice, I see their business take off and their stress lessen. At first, most business owners think their stress will increase because of the time and energy they envision one-on-ones consuming. But after learning how to conduct these sessions consistently and productively, they come to share my belief that these conversations are bridges that can move an employee as well as a business from mediocre to magnificent.

How a one-on-one keeps the conversation going

A one-on-one provides a regularly scheduled opportunity for an employee to talk with the business owner or manager about issues that affect the employee's performance and attitude. Great ideas that benefit the entire organization can also surface in these confidential and personal conversations. There is no one right way to have productive one-on-ones, and leaders need to find the approach that works best for each team and workplace culture. When you commit to making one-on-ones consistent and productive, you will find they:

1. build trusting relationships and loyalty;
2. provide regular checkpoints for accountability conversations and follow up;
3. give you an opportunity to coach employees;
4. set the tone and allow time for mutual feedback from employee to leader and leader to employee, often generating new energy and ideas for the business;
5. are *proactive*—they give you a chance to anticipate and address issues instead of only reacting to problems after they occur.

What keeps one-on-ones from happening?

The two most common reasons for avoiding one-on-ones are confusion about how to make them meaningful and productive and finding the time to schedule them. The key to making these conversations meaningful is to create a consistent framework for how they will be conducted. This standardization will help ease your stress about planning for them. Consistency will also enable you to stick with your commitment to have one-on-ones because it will reduce the pressure to do a lot of planning for each individual conversation. Within a consistent framework, the meetings will unfold naturally and in a mostly predictable pattern. Although there's no one perfect formula for one-on-ones, the components listed below will help in getting you started. Once you've selected the components you want to use, then begin your very first one-on-one with each employee, start with an overview of the process you will use and how these conversations will help you, your employee, and your business grow and succeed.

After your initial one-on-one with an employee, select from the following components to create your consistent framework for subsequent one-on-ones.

- **Celebrate:** Start by having the employee share what's been going well since the last one-on-one. This cultivates a habit of recognizing and appreciating what's working well and gets the conversation off to a positive beginning.

- **What's important:** Find out what's important to the employee by asking, "What's important for us to discuss today?" This is where you need to listen carefully and calmly because you might be blindsided by what you hear. (Chapter four provides tools for both receiving and delivering feedback.) Some leaders like to start with the what's important question. If you don't start with it, be sure to balance the talking time to equally cover both your agenda items and those of your employee.

- **Review data:** Sit side by side and review current data together by asking, "What is the data telling us about our product sales (or whatever data you plan to monitor)?" Be careful not to do too much talking here so you can draw as much as possible from your employee. Your purpose is to get him or her to create a habit of thinking about the numbers when you're not around to ask the question.

- **Choose a goal:** Work with your employee to set a goal from the data or from some other aspect of the employee's performance. Be sure the goal is measurable and observable. You and the employee will both know the goal's benchmark when you ask, "So, how will we know how you're doing with this when we review your progress at our next one-on-one?"

- **Coach:** When an opportunity arises to coach your employee, be ready to shift into coaching mode. By being a coaching leader you can help your employees embrace change. (You can find more on coaching in chapter seven.)

- **Commit and leave with a plan:** Determine what you each will commit to accomplishing between this meeting and the next. Here are some questions that will help you both make strong commitments: What will you commit to doing? What's the first step you need to take? What might get in your way? What support/resources will be helpful? What is your time frame for this? Be sure to leave with a plan that also shows how *you* will support your employee's commitments. Perhaps you will check in via email or be available to talk if the employee encounters a roadblock. Then make sure you follow up at the next one-on-one to see how your employee honored the commitment.

- **Keep a record:** Devise a method to track each one-on-one so you can revisit the progress in your employee's plan at the subsequent sessions. Some of my clients use a small notebook for each employee and simply put the date at the top of each page and jot the commitments the employee makes. The record keeping method you select doesn't matter. Sticking with your chosen method does.

Once you decide to commit to regular one-on-ones, the next step is honoring that commitment. Starting and stopping one-on-one meetings is worse than not starting them in the first place because the inconsistency will erode trust rather than build it. Most of my clients find they honor their commitment to one-on-ones best when they put them on their schedules or delegate scheduling them to an assistant.

Although having one-on-ones will take up time, their value lies in reducing the time currently devoted to putting out fires and reacting to problems as they crop up. Avoiding one-on-ones ends up consuming more time in the long run. Whether you are a supervisor, manager, or business owner these techniques, when consistently used, can cultivate a turning point in your leadership and result in improved performance for your team.

Is "Never Stop Improving" Smart Advice?

Many leadership books use buzzwords like "continuous improvement" and "set the bar high." In theory, the notion of constantly striving to help your employees and business be the best they can be is a good thing. But there are times when improving too much can be too time consuming and too demanding for everyone.

While I was recovering from the devastation of Hurricane Sandy, for example, my views on constant improvement became clearer to me. In preparing for the storm, my husband and I moved about 90 percent of the contents from the garage and ground floor office to the second floor where they would be safe from the flood waters. For the nearly eight months that our rebuilding took, our home looked as though we were still moving in. Golf clubs and garage tools lived in the living room corners. Packed boxes cluttered every wall of every room nearly reaching the ceiling; the dining room table held a mound of coats. Lowe's tagline, "Never Stop Improving," which was plastered on the sides of all those boxes, started to haunt me. I kept wondering if that was really such smart advice.

It's easy to see why Lowe's wants us to believe that tagline: For them, more improving equals more shopping equals more earning. But how helpful is it for leaders to adopt this point of view? How do leaders know when things have improved enough?

First, you need to identify what you want to improve. Is the goal a procedure, an outcome, an attitude, a skill, or a relationship? When you are clear about what you want to improve or see your employee improve, you have a better shot at knowing when you have accomplished the goal and when to stop trying to improve on it further.

Imagine Tina has been with your company for six months and is the cause of many customer rants on public business review websites. It's clear to you that she needs to improve her customer service skills and attitude. You coach

Tina in one-on-ones and invest in sending her for training because you want your customers to feel valued and your business to flourish, and Tina can help accomplish that. With all of this effort, Tina increases her positive customer interactions by about 30 percent, but she still shows up to work in a rotten mood at least once a week.

Because you like Tina, you have invested time and money in hiring and training her, and you may think continued training is the answer. But you may become so focused on the "Tina improvement plan" that you miss the signs that she just isn't going to improve any more in this area despite your efforts. She just isn't right for the position she's in. My point is a "Never Stop Improving" attitude can camouflage a bigger issue so you don't see it clearly.

Second, you need to know when good enough will suffice. Constantly aiming to improve without viewing the goal in a proper context can be counterproductive. Imagine that you are training for a big race and you want to trim a few minutes from your running time, so you add sprints and increase mileage. The next thing you know, you've got shin splints and the doctor says it's from overtraining.

Striving to achieve a highly functioning, productive team for your business is worth the effort, but keep in mind that "Never Stop Improving" can be a good idea gone bad. Improving may be good, but never stopping may be bad. When you are aware you have achieved your goal, you'll be able to stop before you slip over the over-improvement edge, which is smart for you, your employees, and your company.

Teach Expectations to Reach Expectations

Even when expectations are valued and you have made them crystal clear, there will be times when your team doesn't reach the goals you've set. Taking the time to examine what they are doing instead of what you expect them to be doing will reveal where your expectations have gone awry. You may find you dropped the leadership ball or have been a little less clear than you thought. Once you've defined the places where the staff's behavior and your expectations don't match, you'll begin to see the importance of teaching them what you *don't* expect.

Here are two examples of how a lack of clear expectations plays out in the workplace:

A coaching client was completely frustrated with getting her team to adhere to a dress code of stylish and hip attire. She knew how she wanted them to dress, but she had several employees who didn't get it. Although she took the time to communicate this expectation, she felt annoyed when some team members showed up poorly dressed; her version of hip and stylish was translated into their version of artfully torn tops and belly exposing shirts.

During a coaching session, she realized she had let her employees know only what she did expect, rather than clarifying what she did *not* expect. Clothing choices are rather subjective, so to deal with this tricky territory, she decided to show them the dos and don'ts of her expectations. She created a slideshow with images of appropriate and inappropriate attire, and after viewing it, her team began to show up with the type of look she was after.

Here's a second example of how to teach expectations that will sound familiar to both business owners and managers.

Connie is the manager of a service-oriented business with two locations. That meant two teams to hire, coach, and lead. Having two teams contributed to one of Connie's biggest challenges because when she was at one location, the employees at the other location were on their own. Sometimes this meant the right things happened when she was there but didn't happen when she wasn't there.

Connie's stress was high—on a ten-point scale, she rated her stress at a nine or ten. The business owner, Rob, was equally stressed. One day Connie was crying and saying, "Nobody is listening to what I'm telling them to do," Rob told me during our phone conversation. But he was unsure of how to relieve her stress.

In my first coaching session with Connie, we discussed her frustration with the staff not following a new trash procedure. She had initially told the team to leave the trash by the back door. Several months later Connie rethought this decision. She established and communicated a new procedure which was to deposit the trash in the outside dumpster at the end of each shift and not leave it by the back door. For the first few days of this instructed change, Connie would come in each morning to a pile of trash bags by the back door. So, she would tell the employees to take out the trash at the end of each shift again. And again the bags didn't seem to make it to the dumpster in the parking lot.

This may seem like a simple problem, but it's the kind of problem that can drive a manager crazy. "Why don't they just do what I tell them?" Connie said. It felt to her as if they were disregarding her directions on purpose or perhaps even as a challenge to her authority.

During our coaching session, I asked Connie about personal changes she had made herself and how much time it took for those changes to stick. As she reflected on her life, Connie had her first coaching "aha" moment, realizing that she couldn't just tell people to do things differently – she also needed to teach them.

By the end of our coaching session, Connie had embraced the notion that change is hard and it might be possible her employees weren't forgetting to take the trash out to spite her. Maybe they just needed a reminder. To test out this theory, Connie added her humorous touch and left a catchy sign by the back door with huge eyes popping out that read, "I don't see a trash can here."

Much to her surprise, the trash bags were never left by the back door again. Connie was learning that her team wasn't going against her intentionally—they just needed a bit more help to remember new procedures.

This was the beginning of Connie's journey to managing a business with less stress. She recalls, "Back then, I was stressed at home about my job. Now when I go home, work is never on my mind in a stressful way." As the mother of two young children, she could see how having less workplace stress was improving her life outside of work too. Two years after our first session, Connie rated her stress at about a four or five, which was half of what it used to be.

As Connie and I continued to work together, she continued to learn how to identify what it took to help her team grow and how she could affect their growth by using a positive rather than a punitive approach. Connie adds,

> *I'm much better at letting people know how their behaviors or their actions impact me and how I see them. And I let them know what I expect to change. Before I was timid and would hold it in and not say anything. I now confront the situation*

or issue head on every single time, even when I don't want to. I know I have to or I'm holding on to resentment that gets stronger. I still have anxiety before I approach someone, but as soon as I do, I feel so much better. Once I've talked with them I realize it has nothing to do with me.

When you consider the expectations you set for your team, what areas keep getting trampled on? Examine whether those areas could be related to how you are teaching—or are not teaching—your expectations. By clearly communicating what you *don't* expect, you may find you get more of what you *do* expect. When you teach expectations, you can help others reach them.

FOUR

Open the Door to Feedback: Practice Four

Some people say you need to develop a thicker skin to deal with mean people. I think it makes more sense to develop a stronger heart.

—Gayle Luster
Author and Psychotherapist

Feedback between leaders and workers is the lifeblood of a healthy business. Practice four will help you develop skill in giving and receiving feedback and show you how to create a strong feedback culture in your workplace. This true workplace story offers an example of opening the door to feedback.

After having her own business for fifteen years, Shay took a job with a local company. She entered a workplace where most employees had been there for many years—except for the new manager who hired Shay with the hopes of breathing new life into an established business.

Naturally enthusiastic, highly creative, and a hard worker, Shay was filled with ideas for growing the business and improving the workplace. Although Shay was impressed with the top-notch customer service training she received at the company, she saw that the company lacked clearly defined responsibilities or expectations for teamwork. After owning her own business, Shay could see how the company was functioning well in many ways but was not functioning well in other ways.

Shay had been hired for her expertise, yet she found her workmates cutting off her ideas at every turn. Every initiative she undertook was met with, "That's not how we do it here." This made for a frustrating start to her new job.

From her first day of training, however, the leadership team had invited Shay's opinion, and her meetings with them often ended with an invitation to keep them informed of what was working for her and how they could help her perform her job better.

When Shay's six-month review arrived, she felt safe in honestly describing on a detailed feedback questionnaire the challenges she had been experiencing.

About a month after submitting her feedback, the owner of the company invited Shay to meet with him. During their nearly two-hour conversation, he asked thoughtful questions and, more importantly, listened intently to Shay's experience. Six months later there was a new mentoring and orientation program in Shay's company—thanks to her courage in speaking up—and her leader's courage in asking for her feedback.

Think about this story in relation to your business workplace culture. Do you know what your employees actually think about the environment, the procedures, and your leadership? When was the last time you really asked them? Would they tell you the truth if you did ask? How well do you listen to what you hear? What, if anything, changes once you do receive feedback? Like many business owners, you may be afraid to ask these questions for fear of what you may learn, especially when the feedback might be about your leadership—or lack of it. Since leadership style is typically the least talked about topic inside the workplace and the most talked about topic in the parking lot, it takes frequent invitations from business leaders, along with nonreactive listening, to bring this topic into the open.

Shay's success story can be replicated when you maintain an open door policy, not just for your office, but also for the way you invite and receive feedback. Here are five tips that can help.

1. **Ask often**: Invitations for feedback need to be repeated so people have multiple opportunities to provide it and begin to believe you really do want to hear what they think.

2. **Ask specific questions**: Rather than saying, "Tell me what you think," employees might be more willing to respond when your questions are a bit more specific. Try these (or similar) questions: What's working well for you? What is making it harder for you to succeed? What can I do to support you?

3. **Listen fully:** As John Marshall, Chief Justice of the U.S. Supreme Court (1801-1835), said, "To listen well is as powerful a means of communication and influence as to talk well." When you listen fully, you can better understand an employee's point of view. You can then be more thoughtful in your response and ensure the employee feels heard.

4. **Be open:** When you listen with curiosity, rather than with defensiveness, you have your best chance of seeing the employee's perspective and recognizing what needs to change. Stephen Covey said this best, "Seek first to understand, then to be understood."[1]

During feedback conversations, learn to ask, "And what else?" often. This will help you hear your employees' deepest issues and thoughts.

5. **Act:** When leaders invite feedback and nothing changes, the conversations and criticism will move out of the workplace and back to the parking lot. Taking action based on feedback is what keeps the door to conversation open.

When you learn to invite feedback, listen deeply, and respond with action, you will create a feedback culture that improves your workplace and decreases stress for everyone, especially you. After six months of coaching, my client, restaurateur Richard Bach shared this insight,

> *Giving and receiving feedback used to be hinged on emotion. We've been training to get rid of that emotion so it's actually now enjoyable getting to these conversations.*

Give More Positive Feedback Than You Think Is Needed

Have you ever made suggestions for employee improvement only to hear, "Why are you always criticizing me? Don't you ever have anything good to say?" This is an example of getting some difficult feedback in return. Your employee may be trying to say you exhibit the wrong ratio of positive-to-negative interactions with him or her.

Marriage expert John Gottman suggests the healthiest relationships strive for a magic ratio of five positive interactions to one negative interaction and a lack of that ratio in the marriage is a strong predictor of divorce.

I have found that a 5:1 ratio is also valuable when it comes to feedback in the workplace. You might be thinking, *Why should I have to thank people for doing their jobs?* Or you may be the kind of person who requires little praise from your superiors. But most people need a kind word of acknowledgement to be able to maintain their stamina and commitment to their work. Recognition doesn't have to be a splashy show; small and frequent acknowledgements of a job well done are typically more effective. An unexpected thank you, especially from the manager, owner, or leader, is always appreciated. Many years ago I hosted a colleague's farewell party in my home. About a month after the party, I was pulling a box of cereal off the shelf in my kitchen when out slid a blue card from one of my colleagues with a handwritten note of thanks. This happened almost twenty years ago. The fact that I remember it so vividly is a testimony to its impact.

Giving positive feedback does not mean you are constantly lavishing people with praise; however, too frequently offered praise can lose its impact. In *Punished by Rewards*, by Alfie Kohn, an education and parenting expert and author, writes, "Praise isn't only about approval; it's more about letting people know how they're doing, with information they can use to continuing [sic] doing well."[2]

Whether acknowledging someone in person, via email, or by a written note, here are five tips for giving positive feedback.

1. **Make it genuine.** People can spot insincerity a mile away.
2. **Give it privately.** Deliver personal appreciation privately and group appreciation publicly.
3. **Be specific.** Instead of saying, "You really wowed that client," it would be more meaningful to say, "You made a personal connection with that client by remembering to ask about his mother's health. That's sure to inspire loyalty."
4. **Separate positive feedback from confrontation.** When you use the sandwich method—saying something positive, then slipping in something critical—people hear only the negative part. So, it's best to deliver positive feedback as a separate conversation. Note: This positive feedback is different from the positive celebration at the start of a one-on-one since that positive feedback is elicited from your employee—not delivered by you.
5. **Focus on process, not just outcomes.** Instead of saying, "Way to go for making that sale," it would be more effective to say, "Way to

go for hanging in there and persevering." By acknowledging the actions people take, you help them recognize how they contribute to their own and your business's success.

If this amount and type of positive feedback sounds new to you, it might take a concerted effort to shift your ratio toward putting more emphasis on positive rather than on negative feedback. When you find a way to make giving positive feedback habitual, the process eventually becomes automatic and an integral part of the way you lead. Here are some additional ideas for making positive feedback a regular habit. Decide which ones will work for you, then try them.

- Set aside the same time each day or week for writing positive feedback notes.

- Select one day of the week when you offer positive feedback, in person, to your team.

- Remind yourself to find the good and look for it regularly.

- Put reminders on your phone or calendar to help you cultivate this new habit and mindset.

Last, and perhaps most important, before offering critical feedback, first ask, "When was the last time I told this employee something positive?"

Take the Leadership High Road

At times you may encounter employees who are resistant to feedback. They give you the cold shoulder, spew anger, or storm off when you try to initiate a conversation. What's a leader to do when an employee shuts down communication? Take the leadership high road. When you're the leader, it's essential to move beyond grudges and the need to be right. When an employee shuts down communication, ask yourself, "What is the most important thing here?"

You get to decide whether it is more important to win the argument with a commanding communication style or aim to maintain a productive working relationship. Back in chapter three I talked about the importance of conversation and relationship. If you have an employee who is not talking to you, there is no conversation; therefore you have no relationship. And you cannot lead without a relationship.

If you receive occasional resistance to your feedback, that is one thing, but if you notice a pattern of an employee not receiving your feedback well you have entered an entirely different arena. An unwillingness to receive (or accept) feedback may be an indication of someone who is not willing nor able to grow. Chapter five offers specific suggestions for this type of situation since aversion to feedback may be a strong indication the employee is not the best fit for your business.

If, on the other hand, you choose to invest in the employee, then you will want to initiate what John Gottman calls "a repair attempt."[3] Restoring a relationship is not as easy as rebooting a frozen computer; however, it takes courage, skill, timing, and a clear commitment. Once you do resume talking with your resistant employee, you will find your frozen relationship begins to thaw. By reestablishing dialogue, you'll be reestablishing the relationship with the goal of having it function at a higher level.

Here's a workplace example of taking the high road in action. I once had an employee, Diane, who disagreed strongly with me and expressed her views in a demanding tone at a meeting. I engaged in a heated dialogue with her—in front of the team. The next day, she passed me in the hall and responded to my friendly, "Good morning," with a vacant stare. I realized I had some work to do. Here are the six actions that helped me restore the relationship with Diane.

1. **Leave some space.** It's okay and often wise to leave some space between you and your employee—but it's not okay to give someone the silent treatment.
2. **Initiate the conversation and be persistent.** Make the first move. I sent an e-mail to Diane that said I valued our relationship and wanted to talk about what had happened. She replied, "Oh, I don't

need to talk." It took two more attempts on my part until she agreed to a conversation. I could have played the boss card and demanded a meeting, but that felt too forceful and counterproductive to my goal of having a mutually trusting relationship.

3. **Level the playing field.** When Diane finally agreed to talk, I suggested we meet on her turf, rather than in my office. Thus, when we did meet, it helped level the conversational playing field by creating a safe space where she could feel more comfortable.

4. **Own your part first.** Let the employee know what role you played in the conflict. I apologized to Diane for reacting so emotionally in front of others. I acknowledged that had I demonstrated curiosity about her point of view in response to her demanding tone, the interaction would not have deteriorated as it did. When you go first in your repair conversation, you demonstrate courage, commitment, and authenticity and that spirit invites your employee to mirror your actions by doing the same.

5. **Let it go.** There should be no grudges in the workplace. Get over what created the hard feelings and move on. Everyone has bad moments. It's best when you can show compassion for everyone's human qualities, including weaknesses, and embrace the hope that growth can emerge from every conflict.

6. **Don't take it personally.** Don Miguel Ruiz, author of *The Four Agreements*, writes, "Don't take anything personally. Nothing others say and do is because of you. What others say and do is a projection of their own reality..."[4] Cultivating a don't-take-things-personally mindset is one of the most significant ways a leader can learn to take the high road.

As the example with Diane shows, in-the-moment feedback (such as occurred in the team meeting) can challenge a relationship. If you are in the habit of blurting out thoughts and have a mostly critical perspective, it takes work to deliver feedback so it will not be hurtful. To explore the first step above in more detail, here are five in-the-moment feedback examples. Which of the following hold the potential for being helpful, and which could be hurtful?

1. The yoga teacher says, "Let the energy flow through your strong arms."
2. You yell, "Stop!" when you see a toddler darting into the street.
3. An employee is explaining something to a client, and you interrupt to explain it in a better way.
4. Your assistant affixes file folder labels off-center and you say, "Hold on, those need to be centered on the folder."
5. A teacher is in the midst of giving a lesson and you pull her aside to offer a suggestion.

I have given or received the type of feedback in each of these examples. I learned that the first two were helpful and the last three were hurtful. Although my intention in all of the examples was to be helpful, I needed to figure out what was making some of my in-the-moment feedback hurtful. I've since learned how to decide whether to offer feedback in the moment or hit the pause button and plan for a better time to provide the feedback. It's a no-brainer to stop a toddler from getting hit by a car by shouting, "Stop!" Clearly, in-the-moment feedback is helpful when the issue is safety, urgency, or something of grave importance.

In-the-moment feedback can also be a helpful learning tool, as when my yoga teacher gently adjusts my arms, reminding me to extend them fully. Her prompting helps me remember to do so on my own. This kind of feedback is also essential when expressing acknowledgement and gratitude as in, "Thanks for getting that mailing out so quickly. It means a lot to know I can count on you."

In contrast, in-the-moment feedback can be hurtful when the timing isn't right. Many people have a strong preference for receiving feedback that occurs out of the moment. For example, I once privately offered critical feedback to a teacher about her lesson as I was heading out the door of her classroom. The next morning I received an email from her. She let me know how my feedback consumed her thoughts for the rest of the day and asked that in the future I hold off on in-the-moment feedback and wait until the end of the day so she would not be distracted by it while teaching. I felt grateful that my employee let me know how she wanted to receive feedback and especially how the way I delivered it created a negative impact on the outcome of her great teaching—something she and I both valued. If your employees aren't offering you this kind of constructive information, ask for it. People differ in how they want and can hear feedback, and a skillful leader learns and respects those differences.

Another time to withhold feedback is when your emotions are strong or negatively charged, as I described in my interaction with Diane. Wait until you calm down so your tone can be even and non-blaming. As psychologist and best-selling author Harriet Lerner says,

> *When emotions are running high, timing and tact are precisely what make honesty possible.* [5]

Learner also says, "Breathe now, speak later." Taking a breath can give you a different perspective on the situation, as I described in my conversation with Diane. Time will give you a chance to reflect and recognize there are two sides to every issue and that you own part of the problem. Here are four ways you might have contributed to the unpleasantness.

1. You didn't delegate the task clearly. You may have assumed your employee knew more than he or she did. You'll find more about delegation in chapter six.
2. You haven't taught your employees why it's important to explain or do things a certain way. Without emphasizing why a task matters, employees won't place the same value on the task as you do.
3. You're micromanaging. If you have a habit of swooping in and managing every detail, your employees may be learning to let go of the task and leave it to you to eventually clean up.
4. You're more concerned with being right or showing what you know than with supporting or helping the other person.

These are all good reasons to hold off on giving feedback until you have taken some time to reflect and thoughtfully decided how and when to proceed.

Whether you decide to give feedback immediately or at another time, be aware that some people may feel deflated by what you say. That effect becomes compounded when leaders and others avoid crucial conversations because of their own discomfort or because they fear making others uncomfortable, too. It's important to learn how to overcome your discomfort and/or fear so you can give employees the feedback that will help them grow rather than result in a feeling of inadequacy. Here are seven specific tips for thwarting your discomfort or fear in giving feedback.

1. **Ask permission first.** Start by asking for permission so the recipient is a willing participant in the conversation. You might try something like this: "I'd like to offer you some feedback; is now a good time?" If permission is given, then follow up with the other tips. If not, ask for a better time, then leave that exchange with a specific time for the conversation. There are instances when you can skip this step, such as during a performance review, since it's clear at the outset that you will provide feedback during the meeting.

2. **Get the tone right.** A matter-of-fact approach works best. Be careful not to add a doom-and-gloom overtone that blows the issue out of proportion. If your personality is highly charged, letting some time pass before providing feedback will assure that your tone does not reflect your emotions.

3. **Select the time and location with care.** In the workplace, it's generally best to offer difficult feedback at the end of the day (as the teacher in my earlier example recommended to me) so the person has time to process his or her reaction without impacting the workday. Feedback should always be given in a private location and on the recipient's turf whenever possible.

4. **Be clear about the issue.** It can be tricky to tease out the issue. Is the issue a troubling pattern, a one-time error, or just your personal pet peeve? Figure this out before you start the conversation. Susan Scott's model for a confrontation conversation suggests

filling in the following sentence to clarify the issue at hand: "I want to talk with you about the effect _____ is having on _____."[6] I've used this technique when coaching business owners and it really works.

5. **Clarify your intentions.** Clearly state what the feedback is *not* meant for as well as what it is meant for. Here's my sample statement you can try. "I want to assure you that I'm not sharing this to blame or criticize you because overall I think you're doing a great job. I'm sharing this feedback with you to help you grow." The authors of the book *Crucial Confrontations: Tools for Resolving Broken Promises, Violated Expectations, and Bad Behavior* call this "contrasting."[7] The term comes from contrasting what you mean with what the other person thinks you mean along with your assurance of what you do *not* mean.

6. **Use descriptive, not judgmental language.** Sometimes just stating what you observe is sufficient. I once supervised a beginning teacher who seemed completely unaware that she used a well-known and not very nice hand motion throughout her lesson. Here's how I gave her this feedback: "I want to let you know I noticed you placed your hand under your chin and flicked your fingers outward about twenty times during the lesson." She replied, "I did?" We both had a good laugh about it and no more needed to be said.

7. **Offer your support.** Ask the person how you could support him or her in using the feedback you just gave in the workplace or offer specific ideas you have about how you might help the person do so.

As you become more comfortable with giving difficult feedback, and developing a more skillful delivery approach, you'll be less likely to avoid conversations you avoided in the past.

Taking the high road in leadership by delivering useful feedback allows you to see the best in people and to summon the best from yourself. Have conversations that help you keep traveling along the high road. Also remember that just as it's challenging to give constructive feedback, it can sometimes be even more challenging to receive it. That's next.

Five Ways Leaders Can Develop a Thick Skin

As a business owner, you know it can get pretty rough out there. People talk about you. They disagree with your decisions. You walk into the staff lounge or break room and the sudden silence gives you a chill. Some barbed comments even find their way back to you when a "helpful" employee just wants you to know what the masses are thinking. And the more public your position, the more feathers you will ruffle.

When I was a novice principal, I received a hateful letter from an anonymous source. Reading it left me shaken and uncertain. Did the letter mean I wasn't doing a good job? Did I need to change the way I was leading? I considered the message as objectively as possible before discarding it. This happened in 1998, but I still recall how this sharp, but non-specific and anonymous criticism, chipped away at my confidence.

In this age of electronic media, and online business reviews, criticism may come in many forms and can quickly multiply with the click of a mouse. Once you get feedback coming your way, you will certainly hear criticism, and you'll need to learn how to develop a thicker skin. It takes practice to learn to deal with disagreement. Learning how to listen without defensiveness will open the door to feedback and foster healthy and direct communication, but you may need to toughen up a bit. That takes practice, patience, and a willingness to engage in, and even encourage, positive confrontation. Here are five tips for developing that thicker skin.

1. **Don't take anything personally.** Remember that those who oppose you or have differing views from yours are behaving within a personal context. Disagreements are best understood when you know what your employees value, fear, and want. This helps you remember the disagreement is not always about you.

2. **Rise above criticism.** Resist digging to find out more or testing the validity of criticism by venting to others in the workplace. Take the leadership high road.

3. **Be open to change.** Often there is a gem of truth in criticism. Be as objective as possible, mine that truth once you discover it, and be willing to change as a result of finding it.

4. **Share with one trusted person.** When you have even one trusted go-to person outside of the workplace who will hold your pain without judgment, you are reminded you're not alone. You will receive the gift of affirmation that you're on the right path and have the strength to continue.

5. **Develop a stronger heart.** When you open your heart to your critics, you develop compassion for the pain they are experiencing and the life they are leading. Developing a thick skin is an essential part of your growth, because you can't put positive energy into leading when you're putting negative energy into worrying about what others think. When you are on the front lines of growing your business, you can be sure you will generate anger in others at times. Maybe you'll have to dismiss an employee people like or limit hours because of a dip in the economy. Whatever the issue, most people are naturally resistant to change and some will stoop to gossip or nasty behavior to help them cope.

Using these five tips will help you to grow a thicker skin. With practice and time, hurts and insults will eventually roll off your back.

FIVE

Ready, Aim, Fire That Employee!: Practice Five

The biggest mistake I have most commonly made, especially early in my career, was not acting quickly enough when I knew in my gut that somebody probably wasn't the best person for a role...So when a manager realizes that somebody is not right for the job... they need to act quickly—not just for their [sic] own success and survival, but also for the overall team.

—Spencer Rascoff
CEO of Zillow

Firing an employee is never easy but can be necessary. Many business owners and managers err on the side of keeping poorly performing employees too long rather than letting them go too soon. Learning to dismiss the right people at the right time and in the right way is key to reducing your stress in this area. This chapter shows you how to develop your firing skill by outlining what you need to consider before firing someone, how to have what's-at-stake conversations with underperforming employees, and how to conduct termination proceedings in the most constructive way.

Communicating clearly about job descriptions; being transparent about your values, expectations, and goals; and offering a thorough orientation and solid training all help to get new staff off to a good start, but problems may still arise. When the honeymoon is over, and although you've kept the conversation going, you may find some employees still aren't performing well. You know something's missing, but you can't put your finger on the problem or stick with an approach long enough to see if what you're trying has an effect. You may have told employees what to do, but they don't do it, or they do only half of what you've delegated. You may have the feeling that something just isn't clicking. These feelings are counterproductive to producing the business results you're after and the workplace culture you want. When your employees are inconsistent, unreliable, and not performing up to your standards, the negative environment will infiltrate every aspect of your business. You need to get ready to make a decision about whether to keep employees or let them go.

Getting Ready: How to Know When an Employee Should Go

Deciding to fire a person from a job is a big step to take, so how can you be sure you're making the right decision? Read the following examples of problem behaviors that may sound familiar, then work through the smaller steps that will assure your readiness to do just that.

> **Jane:** You tell her how you want her to handle difficult customers, explain why it's important, then she does what you discussed—but not exactly. She leaves out a key step and you end up with an irate customer screaming at you and vowing to never return.
>
> **Chris:** You hire him after a thorough search. You take the time to review his job description with him and orient him to the job, but he comes to you a few weeks later confused about his role. You toss up your hands and think *Was he out to lunch during all our conversations?*
>
> **Scott:** You delegate a project to him. He drops the ball on one of the items, leaving a gaping hole that's going to cost the company money.

You confront him with the outcome, but he takes no responsibility and even asks, "Have you talked with Donna about her part in this?"

Mindy: You ask her to display an array of new products. She shops for items and creates a beautiful and eye-catching arrangement. Later she submits her receipt and it's twice what you expected. You're upset with Mindy's inability to stay within budget.

When the first signs of trouble surface, like the problems described here, owners often avoid addressing them because they hope the person will somehow improve on his or her own. If this describes your approach, you'll need to become more proactive. As discussed in the previous chapters, the kinds of conversations you have with employees after they're hired will either help them grow or help you know they need to go. Although almost no one finds these situations pleasant, it's useful to remember that having the wrong employees in your workplace will magnify your stress level and create unbearable workplace tension that drains everyone.

Something is interfering with the performance exhibited by these employees. It might be skill set, potential, or ability. It could be attitude, personality, personal life problems, or communication skills. To approach the performance issues, you'll need to determine if each employee has what it takes to improve or whether you should cut your losses and let the employee go. Before deciding, it's worth considering if there's something you could do differently that would lead the person to become the kind of employee you want.

As described in chapter three, during the honeymoon phase employees are on their best behavior. You may be optimistic that you have hired the right person. But when the signs that the employee isn't meeting the level of performance you had hoped for, you may doubt your decision. Sometimes an employee makes a one-time blunder, but then owns and fixes the problem.

With others, a pattern of trouble emerges. It might be chronic absentee-ism, dress code violations, or a bad attitude. They might meet expectations when leaders are present but opt out when they're absent.

Pretty soon you find these problem employees consuming your mental energy and the issues they create in the workplace invade your thoughts in the middle of the night. You'll need to discern whether investing more time and energy is worth helping these individuals to grow. If you really like them or they start to show signs of growth but keep slipping back into old habits when you stop supervising them, the decision to dismiss them can be even harder.

When my clients' coaching sessions are repeatedly consumed with talk about a particular employee, that's a sure sign changes need to be made. These are the two likely employee outcomes:

- Either the employee responds to your coaching and changes the behavior, which means you keep him or her on, or

- You realize they aren't willing or able to invest in growth, and it's time for them to go.

If the outcome is the latter, you are at the point where you are ready to begin the dismissal process. Having an action plan to rely on will help. First make sure you've offered the problem employee all the support needed to succeed (refer to chapter seven for specific coaching strategies). To do so, ask yourself these questions:

- Have I provided adequate training?

- Have I provided clear expectations?

- Have I provided specific and timely feedback?

- Have I provided effective coaching?

If you answered no to any of these questions, you'll need to go back to the previous chapters and hone your values and your conversation and feedback skills to assure these things happen before you fire the employee. If you answered yes and the employee is still underperforming, then you're ready to take aim. The taking aim stage is where you carefully identify the changes needed and coach your employee on precisely how he or she will change.

Taking Aim: What to Consider Before Firing an Employee

This phase takes courage on your part and you must make it a priority to have a clear conversation with your employee. I like to call this a what's-at-stake conversation. Some people need to hear those exact words. It might sound like this:

> Cameron, we've been talking about the specific changes you need to make in how you promote our products to clients. Your opportunity to continue to work here is at stake. I need to see an increase in your sales by the end of the month, or we will need to have a different kind of conversation and that could lead to ending our working relationship. I want you to be successful and am committed to helping you. So let's talk further about your plan for making this improvement.

As shown in this example, the plan should identify the issue and clearly let the employee know what's at stake. Set a specified time frame to allow for change to occur. If the poor performance continues, then you must follow through by letting the person go. Otherwise, you'll expend more time, deplete your mental energy, infect your workplace culture, and increase your stress, all of which may just postpone the inevitable anyway. Remember that, although it's difficult to let an employee go, the firing process is also part of the life cycle of an organization.

Here are five things to consider before dismissing an employee.

1. **Get clarity about the outcome.** The best time to think about the kind of post-dismissal employee relationship you want is pre-dismissal. When you are clear about the outcome you want, you can work backward to determine what steps will achieve it.

2. **Have a what's-at-stake conversation.** When an employee is dismissed, it should not be a surprise to the employee, except in rare cases of theft or other egregious acts. When you tell an employee, "Your opportunity to continue working here is at stake," the person has a chance to give an entirely different level of attention to areas of improvement.

3. **Create a plan.** Here are three questions to ask yourself (and answer) before embarking down the road to dismissal:
   a) How much time will I give this employee to address the issues?
   b) What evidence will I see to show that the employee has achieved the expected growth?
   c) What documentation do I need to maintain to satisfy the legal parameters of my locale and/or business?

4. **Provide pressure and support.** The phrase "pressure and support" was coined by educational researcher, Michael Fullan, in his book *The New Meaning of Educational Change*. Fullan explains, that "... both pressure and support are necessary for success."[1] When you apply positive pressure, in the form of clear expectations and a sense of urgency, it can lead to increased motivation and effort from your employee. Support comes in the form of coaching, monitoring progress during one-on-ones, and ongoing feedback to maintain momentum. Pressure and support are a powerful combination.

5. **Act swiftly.** When you have devoted ample time to the above steps and don't see the results you have targeted, it's time to make a decision. When you make it swiftly and act on it with care, you will earn the respect of your entire team. You are upholding the values you want to encourage, and others will respect you for it.

Some employees might even ask, "What took you so long?" That confirms that you've made the right call.

During this process you need to keep feedback ongoing and accurate. When you feel you've done everything possible to help an employee succeed, you are better able to take the action needed to let someone go without guilt. You got ready, you took aim, now you know it's time to fire.

Firing: The Termination Conversation

When results aren't evident after you have followed the steps in the previous section, it's time to have the termination conversation. The manner in which you conduct this conversation can have a huge impact on how the conversation goes and how both parties feel when it's over. Bad firings can be like bad break-ups. I know a professor who felt ambushed when fired by an angry email, a business owner who still regrets an impulsive dismissal in a parking lot, and a longtime employee who was marched out the back door without so much as a good-bye. Your goal is to end the relationship with an employee calmly while maintaining a professional and perhaps a personal relationship with the person. Taking a proactive approach and conducting the conversation constructively can avoid ill will.

The following five tips will help you conduct a termination conversation with confidence and clarity.

1. **No surprises.** Ask yourself, "Will this employee be surprised by the termination conversation?" If your answer is yes, return to the steps in the previous sections and follow them.
2. **Find the right tone.** Be clear, kind, and to the point. Anger doesn't belong in a termination conversation. If your emotions are close to the surface, delay the conversation until you can conduct it with a calm tone.
3. **Keep it short.** Less is more. Here's an example of how it might sound:

We've discussed issues with your performance for the past three months and there has not been sufficient improvement. At this time, our professional relationship will need to end. I've enjoyed getting to know you and value your talents; they just aren't the right fit for our business at this time.

4. **Be prepared for a reaction.** When confronted with termination, an employee will likely choose one (or all) of the following behaviors: deny, defend, or deflect. They may say something like, "How can you fire me when I've been working so hard? Terry is the one who keeps dropping the ball—not me!" When any reaction occurs, it's important to stay calm and bring the person back to the message of this conversation, "Today we're here to discuss that your role with our team is ending."

5. **Wish them well.** When ending the conversation, an expression of gratitude and a wish for the person's future success may sound like this: "I am grateful for the contributions you have made, and I wish you much success." Offer something you can do to smooth the transition, such as a letter of reference or whatever feels right to you.

You cannot control how the other person will respond during a termination conversation, but you can control the wake it leaves by controlling your words and tone. When thoughtfully terminating an employee, do your best to leave an emotional wake that is kind, caring, and respectful.

SIX

Delegate or Die Trying: Practice Six

Skillful business owners and leaders often hit a moment of realization when they discover they cannot know everything and do it all. When they build strong teams, with complementary skills, and learn to delegate with clarity, responsibility, and support they empower their people and reduce everyone's stress—especially their own.

—Dennis Sparks, Emeritus Executive Director,
National Staff Development Council

Do you remember the class from school called "How to Delegate"? Me neither, but I sure could have used it. Like many leaders, I wasn't born with effective delegation skills, and I nearly burned myself out as a result. If you don't learn to develop delegation skills, you can become a prisoner of your own business. The I-need-to-do-everything approach guarantees you will have the most stressful job of all your employees. The good news is that you can learn to delegate before your business dies a slow death because you took on more than you could handle well. Keeping your business running well is why the focus of Less Stress Business Practice Six, Delegate or Die Trying, is so important.

Examining Your Beliefs About Delegation

If you find yourself complaining about workload, feel you're in it alone, or have team members who don't share the workload, your beliefs about delegation may be getting in the way of your ability to effectively delegate. Take a few minutes to examine the four attitudes below and their consequences. Then ask yourself if these beliefs describe any of your attitudes about delegation.

1. **"If you want a job done right, do it yourself."** This belief assures you will have more tasks than you can successfully manage, and you will spend more hours working than you'd like.

2. **"The harder I work the more success I will have."** Acting on this belief can result in you leaving work late and showing up early most of the time because you think being at work always is a good thing rather than recognizing when your hard work has become counterproductive. (Revisit "Is 'Never Stop Improving' Smart Advice?" in chapter three for more on this.)

3. **"Every job needs to be done my way—and that's the best way."** This belief reflects perfectionist and controlling tendencies that can interfere with delegation.

4. **"By the time I delegate this to someone, I could have done the job myself."** This belief reflects a focus on short-term versus long-term outcomes and can lead you to overlook opportunities to empower your team.

Although you may want to share responsibility and lessen your workload, beliefs about delegation interfere with those goals by encouraging quick distribution of tasks and decisions using the read-my-mind school of delegation. It goes like this: You picture a project, tell someone to do it, but are disappointed when the result doesn't match your imagined outcome. Sound familiar? If so, learning to share responsibility more and to follow up clearly will help you achieve the results you want while reducing your stress level at the same time. But first you must get in touch with your core beliefs, identify and challenge those that aren't working any longer, adopt new ways to delegate, and commit to delegating more. Delegation provides a leverage point that will help lessen your stress, free up your time, and create a more dynamic and successful team.

How a Delegation Conversation Can Help

The first time I had specific people to whom I could delegate was when I became a school principal, but my delegation conversation usually went like this: "Um, if you don't mind would you do me a favor and..."

I took this approach because delegation made me uncomfortable. At the time, I didn't have a clue about how to identify, monitor, and shift tasks to my staff. I made lots of mistakes at first, but I gradually learned how to abandon some of the beliefs listed previously and gained mastery over the art of delegation. I credit this mastery to a Fierce Conversations workshop, led by Jim Sorensen, who illustrated a model for delegation conversations that shifted my views and gave me the tools that worked for me.

Sorensen asked, "What am I presently doing that is no longer the best use of my time?" and I had no trouble generating a list of tasks and decisions that would free up my time so I could focus on bigger goals. Then Jim proceeded to describe the Decision Tree model.

This model is a simple approach that empowers those you delegate to by clarifying your expectations for the decisions they will make, providing clear outcomes for tasks they will accomplish, and building trust between you and the staff. With this model, you will create a system of accountability and a path for professional growth. Here is the Decision Tree model that was a game changer for me.

The Decision Tree

The Decision Tree model uses the metaphor of a tree to describe levels of delegation. The simple idea is that when you have a clear conversation about the delegation of a task or decision that includes shared expectations between you and the person you are delegating to, mind-reading skills will no longer be needed. Start by picturing a tree in your neighbor's yard. Each level of delegation relates to the leaves, the branches, the trunk, or the roots of the tree and reflects the damage that can befall your business if an action is missed or misconstrued.

Leaf Level Delegation

Leaf level delegation is when the employee makes the required decision or completes the task without the need for your supervision or involvement. There is no need to check with you *before* taking action or to report back to you *afterward*. At this level, you have complete confidence the employee will both execute the task and follow through to the desired outcome while making the best decisions along the way.

Some people find it helpful to think of it this way: Picture a few leaves of your neighbor's tree that you'd rather not have hanging into your yard. You could easily just grab those leaves and remove them, which would not cause harm to the tree and would not impact your neighbor.

Branch Level Delegation

Branch level delegation is when the employee may make the decision or complete the task, but reports the results to you at specified intervals (daily, weekly, or monthly). This enables you to monitor progress along the way and ensure accountability. You feel confident in your employee's ability to make the decision, yet you still want to stay connected to the process and demonstrate your support without letting too much time elapse between monitoring time points.

So, to return to the tree metaphor, picture a small branch of your neighbor's tree hanging into your yard and obstructing your view. You might choose to cut the branch off, but you would probably want to let the neighbor know you have done so.

Trunk Level Delegation

Trunk level delegation is when the employee makes the decision, creates the plan, and reports it to you *first* for your coaching, approval, or alternate suggestions, and *then* takes action. This level gives you opportunities to support your employee along the way while protecting your business from decisions that could cause significant damage.

So, imagine your neighbor's tree growing so large that it drops rotten apples into your yard, killing your grass and making a mess you need to clean up often. You decide you want the tree removed. It would surely cause a problem if you cut down the tree without your neighbor's approval. So you would be sure to obtain permission from your neighbor first.

Root Level Delegation

Root level delegation is when the impact is large enough that it could cause the most significant damage to the organization. This level requires input from many members of your team before any action is taken by you. As the head leader, you are the one who is ultimately responsible for decisions. Therefore, root level decisions are those you take most seriously and must consider their impact on your entire organization.

So, back to your neighbor's tree, if you were using a chemical treatment on your lawn to kill crab grass, and the roots of your neighbor's tree were erupting on your side of the fence, you would need to gather more information from tree experts and from your neighbor to assure your treatment wouldn't risk killing the tree.

To summarize this model, here are the definitions again.

> **Leaf Level:** The employee makes the decision or completes the task and does *not* report to you.
>
> **Branch Level:** The employee makes the decision or takes action and reports the results to you regularly such as daily, weekly, or monthly.

> **Trunk Level:** The employee makes the decision, generates a plan and reports to you *before* taking action.
>
> **Root Level:** You make the decision with input from others.

The Decision Tree Analogy in Action

Here's an example of how The Decision Tree model was applied by one of my coaching clients in a business situation. As you read this example, notice how this process of delegation enables the owner to gradually empower her staff member.

Jane owns a large real estate firm and decides to delegate vacation scheduling to her manager, Chris. Jane reviews the parameters for the decisions, such as the busiest days that are off-limits for vacations and the optimal number of team members who can be off at one time. Jane initially delegates the vacation scheduling to Chris at the trunk level and instructs Chris to email a copy of the vacation schedule to Jane by the fifteenth of each month. Jane then reviews the schedule *before* the vacations are approved.

Over time, Jane becomes confident that Chris is making vacation decisions according to Jane's expectations, so she moves this decision to the branch level. Now Chris makes these decisions and simply emails a copy of the schedule to Jane at the end of each month.

Once Chris demonstrates consistent success with the schedule, Jane recognizes that her involvement is not needed at all. She then moves the decision to the leaf level, with Chris handling all aspects of the vacation schedule without even showing it to Jane.

This example illustrates how Jane is gradually helping Chris assume more responsibility for decision-making while also building trust, enabling Jane to feel completely confident that Chris will follow through on this task as Jane expects. While using The Decision Tree takes longer for Jane to fully delegate the schedule to Chris, the process ensures a higher level of success and long-term learning for Chris. And best of all, Jane can now shift the time she used to spend on the schedule to other projects.

Reading the above example about delegation may give you insight into what is getting in your way and how you can improve your delegation skills. But there could be more interfering with your ability to actually put delegation into practice. This is one of those areas where insight alone may not be enough to bring about the change you want.

Take a look at a second example that shows how a leader uses insight about delegation to get in touch with her fear about delegation, which leads to lasting change.

Tammy is a business owner who wants to hire a manager so she can delegate the jobs that weigh her down. If she has a talented and skilled manager, Tammy envisions she can take herself out of day-to-day operations and focus on driving more excitement for and interest in her business. She anticipates this change will increase her customer base and grow her business revenue while also reducing her stress.

Tammy has hired three managers in as many years, and they have each failed to live up to Tammy's expectations. Each manager's hiring and firing has consumed Tammy's time, drained her energy, and made her more stressed in the process.

A closer examination reveals what is going on here. Tammy is truly trying to have a manager run her business, yet something is keeping this highly valued goal from happening. Is it just bad luck that she hasn't yet found the right person for this job? What could be getting in Tammy's way? Look at what happened with each failed manager Tammy hired.

1. Tammy's detail-oriented personality led her to micromanage her first manager, Hank. Hank's initiative diminished with each micromanaging encounter until he stopped taking any action unless

specifically directed by Tammy. The result was Tammy fired him for his lack of initiative.

2. Tammy gave her second manager, Julia, responsibility for day-to-day management of the team. When an employee had a conflict with one of Julia's procedures, the employee went to Tammy to complain. Tammy insisted Julia alter the complaint process to address the complaint. Tammy's repeated intrusions undermined the relationship between Julia and the team. Tammy finally fired Julia for her inability to manage people.

3. Tammy didn't give her third manager, Margo, clear expectations for her job role and outcomes. Margo thought she was doing what Tammy expected, only to find out later that she had missed the mark. Tammy fired Margo for not performing her job expectations effectively.

These examples show that Tammy didn't spend any time coaching her three employees in a way that would help them become the kind of manager she wanted, so they all stagnated and didn't lead their team members in the ways Tammy wanted. When things didn't go as Tammy wanted, the disconnect caused serious disruption to her entire staff by inflicting constant change and uncertainty upon them.

Why would Tammy express a strong desire for a manager, yet behave in opposition to her goal? The answer lies in Tammy's "immunity to change." Harvard professors, Robert Kegan and Lisa Laskow Lahey write fully about this concept in their book, *Immunity to Change: How to Overcome it and Unlock the Potential in Yourself and Your Organization*. For our purposes here is a brief overview: Immunity to change is a strong force that keeps Tammy right where she is so she can protect some of her deeply held assumptions—assumptions she doesn't even realize she has.

One way to uncover Tammy's assumptions is by imagining how she might feel if she has a competent manager:

1. The team will depend on the manager, not Tammy, leading Tammy to feel superfluous.

2. The team will communicate mostly with the manager, leading Tammy to feel out of the loop.

3. When Tammy spends time in her new and unfamiliar business development role, she will feel uncomfortable, inadequate, and like the beginner she is—feelings that she dislikes, that are unfamiliar, and that make her uncomfortable.

4. When Tammy shares the secrets to her success with the manager, she will feel less special and may experience a loss of power.

If Tammy can learn to look at these feelings and behaviors as valuable sources of information rather than as problems, she can begin to uncover her resistance. Like Tammy, most of us aren't able to see what's getting in our way. That's where help in the form of a colleague, friend, or coach can be useful.

Here are four questions to ask:

1. What am I committed to changing?
2. What am I doing and not doing instead?
3. What do I fear could happen if I make this change? (This unlocks hidden competing commitments.)
4. What are my *big* assumptions? (If….then….)

Let's say that Tammy's answers lead her to realize her big assumption is that if she delegates day-to-day operations to a manager then she will no longer be an integral part of her business. What then? This one realization can enable her to reframe and redefine her role in her business, eventually leading her to delegate effectively so she helps the manager she hires to develop into the manager of her dreams.

Using the Decision Tree framework while simultaneously understanding your own resistance to change will uncover your big assumptions about delegation and set you on a path to using it more effectively. Both you and your team will have greater clarity about who makes which decisions and a clear process for stepping up to the plate and assuming responsibility. This will free up your time and allow everyone to share the workload rather than leaving the burden on your shoulders alone. When you get out of their (and your) way and gradually empower them to make decisions, you build a team that is a thinking, growing, and acting machine.

One additional suggestion is to teach the Decision Tree model to your team. This will reinforce your understanding and give you and your team a common vocabulary and mindset about delegation. Make clear delegation a shared responsibility so when you and your employee leave a delegation conversation, you are *each* responsible for asking, "On what level of the Decision Tree do I (you) have this responsibility?"

Changing your delegation ways takes practice because delegation is a leadership muscle you need to build; it rarely develops on its own. When you shift your beliefs about delegation, identify and overcome your assumptions and fears, and use delegation deliberately on a regular basis, you will be amazed by how much less stress you feel.

SEVEN

Confront Dysfunction so Your Team Can Function: Practice Seven

Communication is both the cause of and remedy for conflict.

—Mary Rau-Foster
Author and Attorney

Every workplace has a unique culture that is functional, dysfunctional, or somewhere in between. While chapter three focuses on how to communicate with individual members of your team, this chapter is about how you and your team communicate with each other and the relationships and culture that result from those interactions.

Negative, complaining, and gossipy forms of communication result in dysfunctional relationships and a stressful culture. On the other hand, when communication is honest, authentic, caring, and clear, it will lead to functional relationships and a less stressful culture. Part of your job as a leader is to spot dysfunctional communication patterns and learn how to handle them. Confronting behaviors that sabotage the culture you are aiming for is a crucial part of what you need to do. Although the idea of confrontation may feel stressful, the truth is you will experience more stress by avoiding it than by learning how to confront calmly, using coaching and leadership skills. Remember that most employees respect a leader who confronts dysfunctional behavior because doing so creates and maintains a safe place for them to work.

This chapter helps you examine your specific workplace culture and gives you the tools to implement Less Stress Practice Seven: Confront Dysfunction so Your Team Can Function (as a collaborative, successful, and learning-oriented group). Here's a review of some communication basics and how certain styles can be functional or dysfunctional.

How Communication Influences Workplace Culture

The communication culture in a business is like a spiral—when it is spinning upward, the leader and team create a cycle of positive relationships, collaboration, trust, and success; the culture is authentic and honest. But when communication spins downward, everyone sinks into a cycle of distrust and disharmony. Here are some examples of the behaviors you might see in a downward spiral:

- Employees speak up only when they are frustrated or not at all.

- Employees express feelings rudely to coworkers who offend them.

- Employees handle problems by gossiping to and about others.

- Information travels through your team indirectly rather than directly.

An upward spiral doesn't avoid difficult communication—it is just executed more skillfully. Some characteristics of an upward spiral include:

- Employees are comfortable discussing, or even challenging, each other and the leader's thinking, process, and procedures.

- Employees speak clearly, calmly, and directly to one another and the leader when conflict emerges.

- Employees resolve conflict without the leader's involvement.

- Employees speak up to defend the culture without the leader's involvement.

- Employees feel safe discussing any topic, even the leader's leadership skills, which they will also openly discuss with the leader.

Every member of your team contributes to whether the communication spiral moves upward or downward. As the leader of your business, however, you play the key role in shaping the culture by serving as a model of positive and clear communication, establishing boundaries, confronting behaviors that contribute to negative communications, and empowering and guiding the team. Confronting dysfunctional patterns of communication in a way that moves the spiral in the direction you want requires knowing how to spot and confront patterns you want to discourage and support the patterns that create a functional workplace environment.

Patterns of Dysfunction

Dysfunctional communication examples are, unfortunately, easy to find. I overheard this conversation in a hospital elevator:

> **Woman:** Did you notice what was happening with the training? Carol's just not training Tony right. I mean, really, Carol barely knows what to do herself.
>
> **Man:** Yeah, I know what you mean.
>
> **Woman:** Well, I'm certainly not telling Carol. She sure doesn't want to hear it from me.

As the elevator rapidly descended, I decided to speak up. I turned to the woman and said, in my calmest voice, "I'm a patient here, and I want the best experience possible. So I would be grateful if you could find a way to speak up about the quality of Carol's training because effective training could really matter to me and to the rest of your patients."

The woman smiled and nodded her head, seeming to acknowledge that I had a point.

In that conversation, I confronted what appeared to me to be a dysfunctional culture in the hospital's training department. I hope I helped the woman see the bigger picture by considering how her failure to speak up might ultimately affect patients because I believe the lack of honest and clear communication, which stems from and contributes to poor relationships, derails a leader's goals and disrupts the ability of the team to function as a well-oiled unit.

When employees tear one another down rather than build one another up, the workplace culture deteriorates, leaving in its wake an underperforming workforce that will likely lead to a sagging bottom line.

A client once bemoaned to me about her $10,000 mistake wondering, "I can't believe no one noticed it or said anything." When I gently asked, "Is there a chance someone did see it and was afraid to speak up?" there was silence on the other end of the phone. That silence implied an environment where employees may not feel comfortable coming to their leader with problems.

These are just two examples of the kind of indirect conversations that may contribute to dysfunction in the workplace. The following sections will help you spot indirect conversations more easily by exploring the consequences of two main dysfunctional patterns: gossip and triangle relationships.

Gossip in the Workplace

Workplace gossip occurs when speech and rumor focus on personal or private events and people rather than on the work processes of your business. Gossip prevents people from communicating directly, destroys relationships, and creates distrust.

You can spot gossip occurring in your workplace when you enter the staff room and everyone falls silent or when you learn from a friend that a valued employee is planning an exit strategy without a word to you.

Consider these next two examples and decide which one is an example of gossip.

> **Example 1**: A colleague stops you in the hall to vent about a meeting you didn't attend, "You won't believe what Beverly said at the meeting."
>
> **Example 2**: You and a trusted colleague leave a meeting and your colleague asks, "What effects will Beverly's comments at the meeting have on this project?"

What's the difference between these two examples? In the first example, you weren't at the meeting so you couldn't gather all the facts, body language, and nuances of Beverly's remarks. Your opinion of Beverly is being colored by your colleague's venting; it's just gossip.

In the second example, you are debriefing a meeting with a trusted colleague so you can better understand the situation. You were both present so you are discussing a situation you each experienced.

This reminds me of when a young woman complains to her mother about her new boyfriend and then gets annoyed when her mother ends up not liking him. Forming judgments based on the views of others can throw a wrench into workplace relationships, making trust an impossibility.

Relationship Triangles

A cousin of gossip is the triangle relationship. This is a common dynamic that sinks relationships as fast as the Bermuda Triangle sinks ships. It's as forceful as a tsunami and can be just as destructive. Triangular relationships emerge in the workplace, in romance, in families—wherever there are more than two people present.

In her book, *Talk it Out!*, Barbara Sanderson describes an unproductive triangle as follows:

> *Usually, unproductive triangles emerge when someone believes that he has been mistreated in some way and does not have a difficult conversation with the person who he believes has treated him badly. Instead, he goes to a third person and complains...*[1]

Here's an example of a typical triangle in a workplace:

Tyler, Kelly, and Maggie are part of a workplace team gearing up for an event. Tyler is venting to his colleague Maggie.

Tyler: I can't believe Kelly. She did absolutely nothing to help with this event. I've been putting in tons of extra hours to pick up the slack from her laziness. Yesterday she was hanging out in the staff room, with her feet on the counter, as if there was nothing to do around here.

Maggie: Hmm...Yeah. I see what you mean. Maybe she just has a lot on her plate right now and is really stressed out.

Tyler: Well, I've had it with her. She never gets it. I am so done!

Later that day Maggie has a few minutes alone with Kelly and says, "Kelly, I want to give you a heads-up that Tyler is having a hard time with your role in planning this event. He got pretty frustrated when he saw you hanging out in the staff room yesterday."

In this scenario, Maggie thinks she's helping work things out between Kelly and Tyler. Instead, Kelly gets annoyed that Tyler didn't come to her directly to discuss his concerns. Tyler, Maggie, and Kelly are each playing a role in a triangular relationship.

Take a closer look at those roles, which everyone involved needs to be able to recognize and understand before they can change their behavior.

Tyler—The Victim: Tyler sees himself as being victimized by what he assumes is Kelly's laziness. He thinks he's keeping the peace by telling Maggie about the issue rather than by confronting Kelly himself. While the outcome he wants is for Kelly to work harder, he may think it's not his job to get her working harder and feel that all he can do is complain about her effort.

Maggie—The Rescuer: Maggie contributes to the problem by rescuing Tyler from resolving the issue with Kelly directly. Maggie's relationship with Kelly is poisoned by Tyler's complaints since Maggie is only hearing his side of the story.

Kelly—The Villain: Based only on Tyler's assumptions about what he judges to be laziness, Kelly becomes the villain. Her relationship with Tyler is doomed because Tyler won't confront her. Thus, she cannot explain what he perceives to be laziness, learn how her actions might be impacting the team, nor have an opportunity to behave differently.

With a clearer idea of what gossip and triangles look like in the workplace, the next question is, "What can you do about them?" There are several strategies I recommend for you as a business owner in order to create a more functional team. But implementing the strategies requires understanding some leadership concepts and skills that can help you coach your employees toward your goal.

How Your Leadership Style Affects Your Team

How leaders choose to speak and respond to issues around team dynamics is a reflection of their leadership style. Highly effective leaders are fluent in the use of a wide variety of leadership styles. Because there is no one correct way to lead, the best leaders match a range of approaches to the varying challenges and employee personalities they encounter. To help you understand the role your leadership plays in your workplace culture I'm going to compare two styles that live on opposite ends of the leadership spectrum: compliance-focused leaders and coaching-focused leaders.

Compliance-focused leaders lead from the top down, charting the path and demanding adherence to rules. It's a my-way-or-the-highway style of leadership. Of course there are times when top down leadership is required. Imagine a lamp catching fire in the office. That's clearly not the time to start having conversations, coaching your team toward a solution, or seeking input, but that's not the type of top down leadership I'm referring to. What I'm describing here is when a commanding style of leadership is executed in an extreme form and leads to an atmosphere where employees fear retribution, feel manipulated, lack trust, feel no sense of power, lose motivation, and band together in armies where they process their options and plot their survival. This forces them to become distracted from producing quality work and use collaboration opportunities to vent, and sometimes even to sabotage.

If you have ever worked for a top down leader, your heart may be beating rapidly from the memory. I once worked for a bullying boss (whom I couldn't even call a leader). In addition to his commanding style, he frequently taunted my group of employees about his intent to move our offices to undesirable locations. His comments were always delivered with a snarky sarcastic bite as in, "Oh, we'll see where your office ends up next year." When I reflect on that experience, I vividly recall how much time our group wasted because it was spent talking about his comments. Would he move us? Where would we end up? Would we lose our ability to collaborate with ease? Of course the move never happened, but the threat distracted us from our work in a big way. And his leadership eventually was the tipping point that led to my departure.

Think over your own experience, or look at your current workplace. What do your thoughts show you regarding how compliance-focused leaders can contribute to a dysfunctional workplace culture?

Now look at the other end of the leadership continuum. This is where you find coaching-focused leaders. These are leaders with authenticity and courage who are not afraid to engage their team in solution-driven conversations. They confront issues, deal with conflict, and use interpersonal skills and coaching tools to help employees succeed and teams to flourish. These are leaders who don't see their employee relationships as a tug-of-war. They know how to lead their team by walking beside them—not by tugging at opposite ends of a rope. They actively demonstrate a we're-in-this-together attitude, and their employees feel supported, learn to be vulnerable and open about their flaws, seek help when needed, admit to mistakes, feel empowered, and receive active coaching and support that enable them to form strong relationships with the leader and every member of the team.

The best news of all is that every business owner, manager, and leader gets an opportunity to choose a preferred leadership style. While you are clearly born with strong leadership preferences, when you develop heightened self-awareness, devote yourself to learning, and open yourself to coaching, you have the chance to change your leadership stripes. I have made this shift and so can you.

The shift begins with you identifying what it takes for you to become a coaching-focused leader. For when you begin to make even small changes, you will create a devoted and loyal team who will become an integral part of your business success.

Read this workplace scenario to get an idea of where you might find yourself on this continuum from compliance-focused leader to coaching-focused leader.

Imagine you supervise a team of ten employees. A bit of drama unfolds between two members of your team. Here's what happens as they review the weekly revenue numbers together:

> **Joan:** Mike, your numbers are off again this week. What is going on? Why can't you get these right?
>
> **Mike:** Gee, Joan, what's the big deal? You're overreacting to a few minor mistakes.
>
> **Joan:** I can't believe you're talking to me like this! I just can't continue this conversation.

Joan, now in tears, goes to speak with her supervisor, Susan. Joan launches into a list of complaints about Mike ending with, "I just can't work with that man another minute!"

Now imagine that you are Susan. How would you respond to Joan's complaints? Which of the responses below is most similar to your style?

- You tell Joan she needs to bring her concerns about Mike to the human resources department.

- You tell Joan, "There's no crying at work! Calm down and go back to Mike and work it out."

- You schedule a meeting with Joan and Mike so you can mediate their disagreement.

- You ask Joan what ideas she has about how to resolve this issue with Mike.

Of course, there's no one right answer to this question. There are times when you will choose to give advice to Joan or handle the problem by talking with Joan and Mike together. All of the above options are worthy. Knowing how and when to use a coaching-focused approach is the key. So, as a coaching-focused leader, you would choose option four because it will likely be the approach that puts the issue squarely back in Joan's lap. Imagine if you started to see that by coaching Joan to confront Mike directly you have an opportunity to help her to fully debrief a difficult collegial interaction. An added bonus is that Joan will feel empowered and be more likely to confront colleagues in the future. She will be growing strong confrontation muscles over time and will leave the conversation feeling overwhelmingly supported and more skilled to face a tough challenge on her own. Remember this additional cautionary note; resist taking sides since you are not hearing Mike's point of view, resist forming an unproductive triangle by giving Mike a heads up that Joan is going to speak with him. Your role here is only as Joan's coach.

So, by developing your coaching-focused leadership skills, you are able to coach Joan toward resolving the conflict herself rather than having her muddle through it alone.

A coaching conversation between Susan and Joan might sound something like this:

> **Susan:** Thank you for the trust you have in our relationship by coming to me with this problem. I can sense how upset you're feeling about this interaction. Would you be OK with discussing it in more depth?
>
> **Joan:** Absolutely!

Susan: Great. I'm happy to help you figure this out and decide how *you* want to proceed. Let's start with what you see as the issue you're having with Mike.

Joan: Well, I just don't want him talking to me with that tone.

Susan: What is it about Mike's tone that's disturbing to you?

Joan: Who is he to tell me to stop overreacting?

Susan: Oh, so you want him to not comment on how you're reacting?

Joan: Yes, instead of making it about how I react, I want him to stay focused on the issue we need to discuss.

Susan: Oh, I see. Are you feeling that Mike is deflecting the issue back to your reaction rather than staying focused on the issue?

Joan: Yes, that's it!

Susan: That's a very powerful insight you just had.

This kind of conversation helps Joan gain clarity about the issue. Here are some additional coaching responses Susan can use that will help her stay in a coaching-focused role and empower Joan to solve the problem herself.

- **Brainstorm Options:** As the coach, Susan might suggest a brainstorming activity to help Joan consider a variety of options. Here's how that would sound: "Would it be helpful to brainstorm a list of options for addressing this issue? We could make a list, then go back and choose an approach. Is that OK?" (Always have the coachee agree to what you are proposing.)

- **Explore Emotions:** Since emotions are often the keys to unlocking our behavior, Susan might consider, "I sense how emotional you feel about this exchange, so it makes me curious about what patterns you notice that trigger your emotions."

- **Encourage Conversation:** Susan could build Joan's confidence by sharing her experience of Mike in this way, "I've talked with Mike about some difficult topics in the past and found him to be receptive. How do you feel about talking with him about this?"

- **Own Your Part:** To get Joan to think deeper about her role, Susan could say, "I've learned that most times I contribute to a situation, even when I think I haven't, and it helps to tease that out. So, I wonder what you think you might have contributed to the dynamic that's happening between you and Mike?"

- **Offer Practice:** Susan wants Joan to leave the coaching conversation with a high level of confidence that she is fully able to follow through. So she could offer a practice opportunity in this way, "Would it help for us to do a role-play of your conversation with Mike?"

- **Choose an Option:** Susan could encourage Joan's full commitment to action with, "Of all the ideas we've discussed what seems to be the best fit for you?"

- **Offer Support:** Susan's ultimate question for Joan's continued growth and success is, "How can I best support you?"

Coaching-focused leaders believe their job is to help team members resolve conflicts independently rather than provide solutions or refer team members to someone else. Coaching-focused leaders choose how to speak in such a way that team members learn to feel safe going to them for guidance and support. This kind of leadership creates a culture where employees can be vulnerable enough to show their flaws, insightful enough to grow from them, and open enough to allow others in to help. As a result, enormous growth becomes possible for the individual and for the organization.

A *Harvard Business Review* article points out the importance of coaching leadership.

> It might seem that a combination of well-defined expectations, performance data, and clearly articulated business rules would be sufficient to help people make evidence-based decisions on a daily basis. Not so! The secret sauce is continual coaching aimed at improving the performance of every individual.[2]

If you need to gain more knowledge and skill regarding coaching leadership, consider reading, attending workshops, or hiring a coach yourself. But in the meantime, there are some strategies you can use to help you coach your employees during periods of conflict that result from dysfunctional communication patterns.

Conflicts and Resolution Strategies

Emotions are generally at the root of workplace conflict, and difficulty managing emotions can cause them to spill out in ways that create conflict and dysfunctional relationships.

The following story illustrates how a lack of emotional self-management might show up in the workplace. Carly, a manager I coach, often complains, "I'm so annoyed with my team. They ask me too many questions and don't stick to what we've discussed."

When Carly's annoyance triggers her strong emotions, she sometimes blows up when asked even a simple question. She reacts rather than responds. During her planned one-on-ones (see chapter three) she can usually manage her emotions and give a thoughtful and calm response, but at other times she can be blindsided when an employee seems to disregard her directions. She then finds herself exploding with an emotional reaction.

Annoyance and other strong emotions generate negative emotional energy that make Carly focused on others instead of being focused on how she could best manage her emotions. Knowing more about emotional responses and learning how to manage them can make a positive impact on workplace culture and, thus, result in less stress for everyone. So what does Carly need to learn?

Managing Emotions in the Workplace

You may have the heard the term emotional intelligence (EI). Many researchers believe our success in work and life is driven far more by EI than by our cognitive intelligence, more commonly referred to as intelligence quotient (IQ). While IQ remains pretty much fixed from birth, EI can be learned.

Dr. Laura Belsten, founder of the Institute for Social and Emotional Intelligence defines EI as:

> *The ability to be aware of our own emotions and those of others, in the moment, and to use that information to manage ourselves and manage our relationships.*[3]

Here are five steps toward EI that can help you and your employees manage not only annoyance, but the range of emotions that may trigger a negative reaction rather than a constructive response.

Step One: *Name your emotion.* When you feel an emotion clouding your response and take a moment to name it, you raise your awareness of the emotion. Just following this one step can be surprisingly helpful.

Step Two: *Make a list.* For a few days and up to a week, take the time to list all of those moments you feel a specific emotion at work.

Step Three: *Identify triggers.* Review the list you made in Step Two to identify the specific kinds of issues or patterns of behavior that trigger your emotions.

Step Four: *Use self-talk.* When you talk through your feelings internally, you can learn to manage your emotions in the moment. Here are some questions to ask yourself: What is annoying me? What am I feeling in my body? Why might this be irritating me? What am I saying to myself? How am I reacting? How do I feel then? What might a better response be? If I chose the better response, how would I really feel?

Step Five: *Create a plan.* Brainstorm alternate ways to respond instead of reacting emotionally. This will help you create new options for behaving differently.

When you commit to making even one small change in your responses, you are on the road to managing your emotions. For example, when she took step two of the five steps just provided, Carly's list of annoyances covered nearly two typed pages. A few patterns jumped out at her immediately. Carly saw the biggest cause of her annoyance was when employees lacked initiative. This showed up in the numerous times her team would text and call her at nearly any time of the day or night to ask even the simplest questions.

As we continued to discuss that point, Carly realized she had contributed to her own annoyance each time she told her team, "I'm here for you, so please reach out any time you need help." In trying to be a supportive leader, she was inadvertently creating a team with learned helplessness as a primary trait.

By identifying her annoyance triggers, Carly discovered there was something she could do about them. Once Carly retrained her team to be more independent, her feelings of annoyance started to diminish. She is now able to respond in more positive ways to her team because the steps she took helped her feel less annoyed by shifting the focus from her employees to herself. She gained personal control and learned that, by identifying what triggered her feelings of annoyance, she could make the choice to change her reactivity to those triggers and plan a more constructive response.

The same steps that helped Carly manage her emotions can help you to manage yours as well, thereby reducing your stress level (and that of your team) and creating more functional patterns of communication.

In *Primal Leadership: Realizing the Power of Emotional Intelligence*, the authors write:

> *Roughly 50 to 70 percent of how employees perceive their organization's climate can be traced to the actions of one person: the leader. More than anyone else, the boss creates the conditions that directly determine people's ability to work well.*[4]

If the leader isn't actively confronting dysfunction, the organization's healthy functioning will be limited.

Stopping Dysfunctional Patterns

As the leader of your business, you have a great opportunity to stop dysfunctional patterns by using two main strategies: (1) gaining self-awareness and self-control and (2) listening and coaching. Let's look at the two main dysfunctional patterns, triangles and gossip, to explore how to apply these two strategies.

Stopping Triangles from Forming

This next workplace example is from a series of monthly training sessions on triangle relationships (and other communication behaviors) I facilitated with a workplace team. In this scenario, notice how a shift in one employee's typical behavior prevents a triangle from forming.

Recall that a triangle typically includes three roles: the villain, who is perceived as causing a problem; the victim, who is perceived as suffering the consequences; and the rescuer, who tries to fix the problem.

> **Jan—The Villain:** Jan's job as the receptionist is to schedule clients for hair appointments. As instructed by the manager, she routinely gives them a forty-five-minute appointment.
>
> **Cindy—The Victim:** Cindy, the stylist, has a new client coming in and needs one hour to ensure time for a full consultation and positive start in building a good relationship with the new client. When she sees she has only forty-five minutes scheduled, she becomes stressed and falls behind with clients for the rest of the day. Her instinct and past behavior is to rush to her manager Donna to complain about Jan's poor scheduling.
>
> **Donna—The Rescuer:** In the past, Donna would have quickly responded to Cindy's complaints and swooped in to reprimand Jan for her lack of understanding about how to schedule new clients.

I had previously coached this salon team about triangles, and Cindy, in particular, had expressed the desire to choose new behaviors. I was fortunate to have had a scheduled coaching session with Cindy on the day this particular conflict occurred. I asked her to imagine what would happen if she brought the problem to her manager, Donna. Here's what Cindy said she imagined could happen:

- Jan would feel reprimanded and blame Cindy.

- Jan would not trust Cindy.

- Cindy wouldn't know Jan's reasoning for scheduling the appointment for forty-five minutes. Maybe something more was going on.

- Cindy and Jan's relationship would be damaged.

Take a closer look at what Cindy did, which illustrates a few strategies to keep these damaging relationships from forming in the first place.

Strategy One: *Gaining Self-Awareness and Self-Control.* The first strategy to use in avoiding triangle relationships is gaining self-awareness and self-control. With coaching, Cindy noticed that by venting to Donna, even though Donna was their supervisor, she would likely cause a triangle to form. Cindy is learning to ask herself some reflective questions (sample questions follow) so she can continue to gain self-control and keep triangles from forming.

- What is upsetting me?

- What assumptions am I making?

- Can I let this go?

- Who is the best person for me to talk with so that I can maintain good relationships *and* resolve this issue?

- What might be the impact of that conversation?

When Cindy recognized her role in this triangle, she was able to stop the behavior that helped to form it. Anticipating the impact of her actions allowed her to explore her response options. Cindy also learned that by waiting a few days to process the issue and calm down, she could better figure out how to address it and do so more constructively.

I mentioned a second strategy, listening and coaching, and I will cover it. But first I want to fill in some information about getting to the point of using strategy two, so read on.

Stopping Gossip in its Tracks

Your workplace will be less stressful and more productive when conversations focus on ideas, strategies, and goals—not on people. Putting a stop to gossip is similar to putting a stop to bullying in that it takes everyone's commitment, everyone's voice, and everyone's courage to do so. You can't deter gossip by yourself, but you can educate your team to create a gossip-free and less stressful workplace.

Here's an example of how one leader I coached tackled the problem. With my coaching support, she took these five specific actions that you can also apply in your workplace.

1. **Clarify expectations:** She put gossip on the table for discussion and set a clear expectation regarding what was and was not acceptable. She included that she wouldn't hesitate to fire someone who continued to gossip.
2. **Act as a role model:** She realized that even by listening to gossip she was condoning it, so she stopped listening when employees shared a juicy tidbit of gossip with her. She instead learned to change the subject or use it as an opportunity to coach the

employee on how to talk with colleagues directly rather than gossip about them.

3. **Help others understand their roles:** She brought gossip out in the open and taught her team that when they listened to gossip, without expressing a desire for the gossip to stop, they too were condoning it. This helped them to see they also had a role in the gossip dynamic.

4. **Identify how gossip impacts the workplace:** She helped her team see how gossip was creating tension, forming cliques, and negatively affecting productivity and teamwork.

5. **Teach triangle roles:** She taught her team about dysfunctional triangles, how to recognize them, what to do about them, and how direct communication can prevent them.

Letting gossip persist in your workplace culture will contribute to triangle relationships. To stop it, you'll need to follow these five steps consistently while you listen to your team and coach them toward more functional communication patterns.

Strategy Two: *Listening and Coaching.* The first thing people tend to do when on the receiving end of gossip is listen to it. Listening is necessary at times, when the other person just needs to be heard, but as leader, you must listen without forming a triangle; you must refrain from agreeing or disagreeing. An example might sound like this: "You sound pretty upset. I can see how this situation adds stress to your day."

The second thing you can do is help the person consider options, which is a key coaching strategy. You can do this by first asking, "Would you like my help with this?" If the person agrees, you can pose questions to help gain clarity, as shown in the earlier example with Susan and Joan. This works best when you withhold your opinion and stay focused on the employee's needs. Here are some additional questions to ask, from the example with Cindy and Jan.

- "What do you think might have been going on with Jan to cause her to not schedule your client for the full hour?"

- "What do you want to do about this?" Then ask,

- "What might happen if you take this approach?" (Then discuss the approach with the person.)

When you help your team talk to the right person, use self-awareness and self-control, anticipate how their actions might lead to triangles, and handle gossip well, you'll start keeping those dysfunctional communication patterns at bay. While the leader's role is key, every member of the team also contributes to the communication culture. Empowering individuals to find their voices and use them in a positive and calm way is essential; it takes everyone in your business to maintain its health and make the choices that do so. Of course, there will still be conflicts. Healthy disagreement and discussion are key ingredients of a healthy culture. It's how everyone handles conflict that matters. And you and your team will be better equipped to handle them well if you follow this chapter's information.

Dealing with Coworker Conflicts

Whose problem is it when employees can't get along? When conflict is not addressed, it becomes an issue for everyone in the workplace because it creates tension that will be felt by the entire team. Some coworker conflict is inevitable, but if you value teamwork and relationships, then you need to send a consistent message: *Everyone will work with everyone. We don't need to be best friends, but we do need to have positive and productive working relationships. That is nonnegotiable.*

As you will begin to see by using several practices in this book, different approaches may be needed for different circumstances. You might choose to mediate the conflict so both parties can truly hear each person's point of view, find common ground, and problem solve together, or you may choose to meet with each person separately. To become a leader who helps to create a safe, healthy, and less stressful workplace for all employees, you'll also need to examine the role you may be playing in any conflicts that arise, especially if you tend to ignore them. Business trainer and author Neil Ducoff writes in *No-Compromise Business*:

> *Left unchecked, conflict between individuals spreads toxic waste all over everyone. Dialogue can lead to resolution. It's the leader's role to be the catalyst for that dialogue, before the situation escalates. Leaders cannot ignore interpersonal conflict.*[5]

Consider Kathy, a client I coach, and the actions she takes in this example, and compare them with what you would do. Kathy has two employees in conflict. Their bickering escalates and is affecting customers, who see the eye rolls, hear the nasty tones of voice, and feel the tension between the coworkers.

Kathy wonders if she needs to redo the work schedule and separate the employees' shifts. That would be an easy fix that underscores the position that these two employees should not work together. Instead of separating the two, Kathy decides to give it time and see if their dysfunction works itself out, but the conflict grows more intense each day.

Kathy has a good relationship with Rick, the business owner, so she reaches out to him for support, and they brainstorm some possible solutions. They hit upon a novel idea, and Kathy decides to give it a try.

Kathy's Three-Step Approach

1. **Kathy meets with both employees together.** Kathy clearly and calmly explains what is at stake (see chapter three) by saying, "Your conflict is creating tension in our workplace and it's even impacting our customers. It can't continue. If you can't work well together, then I will be in a difficult position and need to dismiss one or both of you. I value your work with our company and hope it doesn't come to that."

2. **Kathy helps their conversation succeed.** Kathy reminds the employees of a communication tool she has previously taught them—The Five Words (see chapter three for more on this). By using the

template of these five words: *When You...I feel...Because,* she encourages the employees to express their points of view without blaming the other person.

3. **Kathy shifts responsibility for a solution to the employees.** Kathy and Rick put money behind their beliefs and give the two women $50.00 plus time to leave work and talk with each other over a meal. Kathy sends them off with this charge, "I am confident you can understand each other's point of view, resolve your conflict, and find a way to work well together when you return."

Kathy shared with me later, "It felt like I was entering a burning building when I talked with them, but I told myself it would feel better after I addressed their conflict directly." And it did. Kathy could feel an immediate change when the women returned from the restaurant. Best of all, their positive interaction has continued since.

Kathy and Rick's creative approach is not meant to solve all workplace conflicts—but it is something to consider. When I complimented Rick on their solution, he joked, "The next day eleven other employees showed up professing hatred of one another so they could get a free meal."

You can help employees have positive relationships by setting expectations, shifting responsibility, teaching conversational tools, and expressing confidence in their power to resolve the issue. You deserve and can have a workplace where people learn to resolve their conflicts and get along. But it's not always easy to stay calm in the face of conflict.

How to Stay Calm in a Difficult Conversation

Many leaders avoid difficult conversations out of fear of becoming overly emotional. Employees also become skilled at stuffing feelings and carrying on as if everything is fine—even when it's not. Avoiding difficult conversations can lead to high stress levels because avoidance consumes a lot of social and emotional energy and holds you and your team back from resolving some tough problems. (See the resource section at the back of the book for a list of resources on the topic.) Learning how to stay calm during these conversations is one technique that can reduce the stress level for you and for your team.

In addition, your own defensive reactions to staff feedback can contribute to conflict in the workplace. If you cannot hear what others are saying and see things from their point of view, you end up inadvertently playing a role in the gossip and triangle relationships that develop. Learning how to have difficult conversations will shift the communication spiral direction upward rather than downward. In this section, I share some ideas on how to do this.

Staying curious. One of the most valuable suggestions I received during my coaching training was the advice to stay curious when listening to a client and to hold off on responding too quickly. Stay-curious became my new mantra whenever someone challenged me with a troubling tone or hard-to-hear words.

Learning to stay curious enables you to avoid becoming defensive or blaming and to stay open to the other person's concerns. Putting your internal thoughts and emotions on the back burner for a few moments leaves the space to really hear and take in another person's point of view. It will help you stay calm in difficult conversations.

In contrast, trying to convince your employees about the brilliance of your approach, without taking the time to learn what their objections might be, will shut down the employees' feedback. By staying curious, you allow their concerns to surface and be discussed. And you act as a role model for how to stay calm in difficult conversations.

Alison, a spa owner and a client of mine, had been incorporating the stay-curious strategy into her leadership behavior. She was able to stay curious in conversations she initiated but was struggling to do so when blindsided by in-the-moment conflict—until she had this breakthrough. Here is what happened.

One day, Dawn, a nail technician in Alison's spa, arrived at work and found an outside group was conducting an education class. The class, organized by Alison, had replaced Dawn's typically well-organized and calm workspace with chaos. Dawn became immediately agitated and frustrated by this unexpected disruption and lashed out at Alison, shouting, "I can't work like this. This is ridiculous! You should plan better!"

Alison could feel her blood starting to boil in response to Dawn's blaming and public accusations. Alison could feel her emotions rising, but now knew she could either choose her best response or blow-up at Dawn, which would be reacting in her previously typical way. Recognizing that she needed a moment to regroup, Alison retreated to the bathroom for a calm space so she could decide how to proceed. Alison closed the door and reminded herself, "Stay curious. Don't react. Dawn isn't seeing the whole picture. This isn't her fault. I played a role in her reaction by not giving her a heads-up about the class."

After her brief reprieve, Alison found Dawn and said, "I know that everything looks chaotic, and I'm so sorry. I really appreciate your caring about providing the best service for our clients and letting me know how you're feeling."

Dawn replied, "Thanks, Alison, It means everything to me that you care about my feelings."

In my debriefing of this event with Alison, she said, "The more emotionally aware I become, the easier it gets to show up with curiosity first. I realize that my past actions have often been just reactions to others and they don't have to be."

It will be useful to you to find the mantra or behavior that will help you change your own responses. For example, another client remembers to use an approach similar to Alison's by reminding herself, "Don't get emotional—go to the bathroom!"

By staying curious, you'll become a better listener and be able to hear feedback more clearly. Making this one change will help you remember to be fully present in the face of hard-to-hear words and strong emotions.

This chapter ends with an email one of my clients received from a member of her team. This heartfelt message illustrates how the leader's growth in managing emotions and maintaining calm, clear, communication patterns can serve as a model for employees and result in a dramatically improved workplace where employees' emotional safety is valued and productivity soars.

> Thanks for giving us the time and tools to talk. It's great being able to speak freely. It means the world knowing you hear us and help us to hear one another. With every conversation, I feel as if a weight has been lifted, even when we don't resolve or change anything. It's so much easier to go to you now that you don't get defensive. You value my feedback and listen. This has changed the culture here, helped us be more of a team, and made me love my career.

By learning and using the tools in this chapter, your employees can feel this way, too.

EIGHT

Conclusion: How to Get From Here to There

You must do the thing you think you cannot do.

—Eleanor Roosevelt
First Lady of the United States
1933—1945

As you read through this book, you likely discovered some Less Stress Business Practices that are new to you. Some of them may have intimidated or worried you, challenged your beliefs, seemed in conflict with your habits, or may still seem out of reach. But it is my hope that as you've read these pages, you've nodded with recognition and often felt good about your leadership when you've come across practices you were already following, while understanding some may require more skill on your part. Trying a few strategies, then rereading the whole book, or certain sections, may make the ideas presented here become clearer, depending on where you are in the process of developing your business leadership. By improving your leadership skills and putting these practices into place, you will reduce your stress levels and those of your employees.

While you may have moments when you feel you cannot change some of your current practices, you truly can do so. Like most things in life, change starts with you. You are the leader. You set the tone. You model the example. To get from here to there, you have many choices to make. A good place to begin is by answering the question, "Why?"

- Why do I want to improve?

- Why do I want less stress in my business and life?

- Why would I be better off with less stress?

- Why would my business be better off?

- Why would my health be better off?

- Why would my life and family be better off?

When you are clear about why, you will have a focused path to getting started. You can't work on everything at once. That's a sure ticket to feeling overwhelmed and disoriented. Take on one or two new practices at a time and you will begin to see your stress diminish. But if you don't know where you are, you can't get to where you want to go, so I have developed a simple self-assessment that will help you decide where you are now in relation to the seven Less Stress Business Practices.

The Less Stress Business Practices Self-Assessment

The assessment is organized by each chapter topic. As you review your results, you can return to the chapters in this book that offer the most support for the areas you decide to improve.

Read the directions and complete the assessment to help you determine where you need to focus your attention and energy. Afterward, reread the relevant chapter or chapters to help you choose the next steps to take.

Directions:

- Be honest. As you take this introductory assessment, truly reflect on where you currently are in your leadership journey. This is for you and no one else, so make it matter.

- Place a checkmark in the column that best indicates where you are for each Less Stress Business Practice indicating if you use the practice rarely, sometimes, or always.

- Think about how much stress you feel about each practice.

- Then rank your stress from one to ten, with one being very little stress to ten being extreme stress. Jot this number in the column to the far right.

- Review your results and rank each item from highest stress to lowest. The item or items with the highest stress rank will identify those you need to address first.

- Reread the chapter on the particular Less Stress Business Practice you want to incorporate into your leadership growth plan.

Less Stress Business Practices Self-Assessment

Practice 1: Say Yes to Less Stress (Your goal for this section is to gradually reduce each response to rarely.)	Rarely	Sometimes	Always	Stress Rank (1-10)
1 I have one or more signs of stress, such as back pain, headaches, anger, impatience, and disrupted sleep.				
2 I have employees who are inconsistent, unreliable, and not performing up to my expectations.				
3 I feel frustrated trying to get employees to do their jobs in the way I expect.				
4 My business is a constant source of worry, even when I am at home.				
5 I carry conversations in my head and avoid having them with the people I need to confront.				

	Rarely	Sometimes	Always	Stress Rank (1-10)
6 When there's an employee problem, I don't think to ask myself, "How might I have contributed to this?"				
Practice 2: Aspire Higher When You Hire (Your goal for this section is to gradually shift each response to always.)				
1 I check references thoroughly for all prospective hires.				
2 I prescreen applicants to determine which have the most promise for my valuable interview time.				
3 I am clear about the values and skills needed in a new employee.				
4 I seek input from team members throughout the hiring process.				
5 I use a consistent set of well-thought-out interview questions.				

	Rarely	Sometimes	Always	Stress Rank (1-10)
6 — I have key open-ended interview questions that uncover the applicant's attitude, personality, and character.				
7 — I listen deeply during an interview for opportunities to probe with follow-up questions.				
8 — I look for the potential leaders around me and give them an opportunity to grow.				
Practice 3: Keep Talking When the Honeymoon is Over (Your goal for this section is to gradually shift each response to always.)				
1 — I talk with employees as soon as I notice a pattern of problematic behavior, including a bad attitude.				
2 — I have consistent and clear one-on-one meetings with my team that focus on their growth.				
3 — I acknowledge and celebrate my employees' success with each of them.				

	Rarely	Sometimes	Always	Stress Rank (1-10)
4	I provide clear expectations to my staff.			
5	I explain and show employees what I don't expect.			
Practice 4: Open the Door to Feedback (Your goal for this section is to gradually shift each response to always.)				
1	I ask employees for feedback in a way that helps them tell me what they truly think.			
2	I listen to feedback without becoming defensive or reactive.			
3	I make changes in response to the feedback I get.			
4	I have a thick skin and don't take what others say and do personally or emotionally.			

5	I don't blurt out criticisms when my emotions are high.				
6	I consider the best timing, tone, and location for offering difficult feedback.				
7	I'm clear about the issue before giving feedback.				
8	I give difficult feedback with clear, descriptive (not judgmental) language.				
9	When I give feedback, I also support my employees in making changes.				
10	I give five times as much positive feedback to my employees as corrective feedback.				

Practice 5: Ready, Aim, Fire That Employee! (Your goal for this section is to gradually shift each response to always.)	Rarely	Sometimes	Always	Stress Rank (1-10)
1 I have no marginal employees who contribute to my stress.				
2 I don't delay in dismissing a poorly performing employee.				
3 When I fire an employee, other members of the team are not surprised, and feel supported.				
4 I provide adequate training for marginal employees.				
5 I provide clear expectations about what needs to improve for marginal employees.				
6 I provide specific and timely feedback for marginal employees.				

	Rarely	Sometimes	Always	Stress Rank (1-10)
7 My dismissal conversations are short, respectful, and to the point.				
8 When I dismiss an employee, they say, "I knew this was coming."				
Practice 6: Delegate or Die Trying (Your goal for this section is to gradually reduce each response to rarely.)				
1 I complain about my workload.				
2 I believe that if I want a job done right, I need to do it myself.				
3 I believe the success of my business is due mostly to my hard work.				
4 I believe most jobs need to be done my way.				

		Rarely	Sometimes	Always	Stress Rank (1-10)
5	I delegate quickly without giving lots of details.				
6	I assume employees will know what I expect them to do when I delegate a task.				
Practice 7: Confront Dysfunction so Your Team Can Function (Your goal for this section is to gradually shift each response to always.)					
1	I don't react emotionally when challenged by an employee.				
2	I don't listen to employee gossip.				
3	I don't intervene on behalf of my employees so they don't have to confront one another.				
4	I expect all employees to get along and work well with one another, and I support them in doing so.				

5	I choose when and how to express my emotions without withholding those that matter most.				
6	I know which typical employee behaviors trigger an emotional reaction from me and use this information to adjust my behavior.				
7	I help my team learn how to speak up to one another.				
8	I serve as a model for how to manage difficult emotions.				
9	I coach employees on how to handle conflicts with one another.				
10	I confront employees who engage in gossip.				

How To Hire A Coach

You've completed the self-assessment, reread the relevant chapters, and decided what steps to take next. If you feel at this point you would like more guidance on how to implement these practices to lower your stress level even further, consider hiring a coach to help you.

As I was writing this book, I conducted many interviews with my clients, hearing their stories of self-discovery and insight during the coaching process. This helped me understand which strategies and ways of thinking were most effective in diminishing their stress levels and confirmed for me how helpful coaching can be in a business setting. The words of hair salon owner and industry leader, Christine Zilinski, sum this up best and are a reminder from the chapter one story, It's Not a Tug of War. Here is what Christine told me.

> I reduced my stress when I changed my mindset from them to me. I used to always think it was some other problem and not my own issue. I'd say, 'They did this or they did that.' Learning to understand that I can't change other people and can only change myself—by working on myself—made the difference. Once I changed my frame of mind, it changed the whole dynamic with my team. I had read about this in so many books but didn't truly get it until I worked on this with a coach.

What to Look for in a Coach

If you're like Christine and my other clients, you may find your growth accelerated by working with a coach. There are many great coaches with whom you can partner to help you maintain your commitment and accountability to your goals. Here's what to look for as you consider hiring a coach. An effective coach will be able to do the following:

- Help you celebrate your successes while challenging you to grow.

- Listen deeply to understand your point of view.

- Ask thoughtful questions that spark your insight and action.

- Help you consider possibilities that hadn't occurred to you before.

- Help you uncover what is getting in your way.

- Create a safe space where you feel comfortable discussing any topic.

- Provide a return on your investment (ROI).

- Have credentials from the International Coach Federation (ICF; coach-federation.org) that show that stringent education and experience requirements have been met.

Take your time and do some research to find a coach who matches your needs. You can view the ICF website or visit your local ICF-affiliated organization for search tools that will help you locate certified coaches in your area. Here is a brief excerpt from the ICF website that shows how effective good coaching can be.

The *ICF Global Coaching Client Study* shows most clients reported improved work performance, better business management, more efficient time management, increased team effectiveness, and more growth and opportunities.

The same study found that coaching clients noted greater self-confidence, enhanced relationships, more effective communications skills, better work-and-life balance and an improvement in wellness. Nearly 70 percent of *individuals* indicated they had at least made back their initial investment. The median suggests that a client who achieved financial benefit from coaching can typically expect a ROI of more than three times the amount spent.

According to the same report, the vast majority of *companies* (86 percent) say they at least made their investment back. In fact, almost one-fifth (19 percent) saw a ROI of 50 times their investment, while another 28 percent saw a ROI of 10 to 49 times the investment. Nearly all companies or individuals who hire a coach are satisfied. According to the *ICF Global Coaching Client Study*, a stunning 99 percent of people who were polled said they were somewhat or very satisfied with the overall coaching experience.

Whether you choose to be supported by a coach, a colleague, or your own best efforts, as you embrace each Less Stress Business Practice and begin to make them habitual, you will find that they gradually become your default way of operating. With that automaticity, your stress will melt away. Be kind to yourself as you do your coaching. It won't always be easy and you will err at times. But always remember change requires great effort and the ability and practice of forgiveness, not only of others, but also of yourself. That's why I deeply believe people change from a place of acceptance, caring, and even love. People change when they feel good about themselves—not when they are shamed. People change when they know someone is in their corner cheering for them and expecting them to do well.

I'm in your corner cheering for you. When you adopt new practices, make significant changes, and begin to think and act differently as you lead your business, you will find you have less stress than you've ever imagined possible. Please get in touch with me at Jamie@LessStressBusiness.com when you see your first glimmer of transformation. I'd love to hear how you're doing.

Notes and References

CHAPTER ONE: SAY YES TO LESS STRESS

1. Herbert Benson, "Are You Working too Hard?" *Harvard Business Review,* Fall (2011).

CHAPTER TWO: ASPIRE HIGHER WHEN YOU HIRE

1. Jim Collins, *Good to Great: Why Some Companies Make the Leap... and Others Don't.* New York: HarperCollins, 2001.
2. Brené Brown, *Daring Greatly: How the Courage to Be Vulnerable Transforms the Way We Live, Love, Parent, and Lead.* New York: Gotham Books, 2012.
3. Sheryl Sandberg, *Lean In: Women, Work and the Will to Lead.* New York: Knopf, 2013.
4. Lorraine Grubbs-West, *Lessons in Loyalty: How Southwest Airlines Does it – An Insider's View.* Texas: Cornerstone Leadership Institute, 2005.

CHAPTER THREE: KEEP TALKING WHEN THE HONEYMOON IS OVER

1. Daniel Goleman, Richard Boyatzis, and Annie McKee, *Primal Leadership: Realizing the Power of Emotional Intelligence.* Boston: Harvard Business School Press, 2002.

2. Harriet Lerner, *Marriage Rules: A Manual for the Married and the Coupled Up*. New York: Penguin Books, 2012.

CHAPTER FOUR: OPEN THE DOOR TO FEEDBACK

1. Stephen Covey, *The 8th Habit: From Effectiveness to Greatness*. New York: Free Press, 2004.
2. Alfie Kohn, *Punished by Rewards: The Trouble with Gold Stars, Incentive Plans, A's, Praise, and Other Bribes*. New York: Houghton Mifflin, 1999.
3. John Gottman, *The Magic Relationship Ratio*. YouTube, 2007.
4. Miguel Ruiz, *The Four Agreements: A Practical Guide to Personal Freedom*. California: Amber-Allen, 1997.
5. Lerner, *Marriage Rules*.
6. Susan Scott, *Fierce Conversations: Achieving Success at Work & in Life, One Conversation at a Time*. New York: Viking, 2002.
7. Kerry Patterson, Joseph Grenny, Ron McMillan, and Al Switzler, *Crucial Confrontations: Tools for Resolving Broken Promises, Violated Expectations, and Bad Behavior*. New York: McGraw-Hill, 2005.

CHAPTER FIVE: READY, AIM, FIRE THAT EMPLOYEE!

1. Michael Fullan, *The New Meaning of Educational Change*. New York: Teachers College Press, 2001.

CHAPTER SEVEN: CONFRONT DYSFUNCTION SO YOUR TEAM CAN FUNCTION

1. Barbara Sanderson, *Talk It Out!: The Educator's Guide to Successful Difficult Conversations*. New York: Eye On Education, 2005.
2. Jeanne W. Ross, Cynthia M. Beath, and Anne Quaadgras, "You May Not Need Big Data After All." *Harvard Business Review*, December 2013.

3. Laura Belsten, *Social + Emotional Intelligence Certification Program*. 2013.

4. Goleman et al., *Primal Leadership*.

5. Neil Ducoff, *No-Compromise Leadership: A Higher Standard of Leadership Thinking and Behavior*. Florida: DC Press, 2009.

Keynotes and Workshops

Jamie Sussel Turner presents keynote speeches and workshops on the following topics. Customized workshops are also available for businesses and organizations. Kindly forward all inquiries to Jamie@LessStressBusiness.com

- **Say Yes to Less Stress:** Lead and Live with Less Stress

- **Aspire Higher When You Hire:** Create Teams Built to Succeed

- **Keep Talking When the Honeymoon is Over:** Help New Hires Succeed with Communication, Training, and Commitment

- **Open the Door to Feedback:** And Enjoy the Conversations

- **Ready, Aim, Fire That Employee!:** Stop Trying to Turn Childhood Paintings into Rembrandts

- **Delegate or Die Trying:** Figure Out What's Getting in Your Way

- **Confront Dysfunction so Your Team Can Function:** And Your Business Can Flourish

- **Stop Avoiding Authentic Communication:** Tools for Mastering Dialogue

- **What's-at-Stake Conversations:** Learn to Confront Anyone about Anything

- **What's at Your Business Core?:** Create Your Vision, Mission, and Core Values

Client Testimonials

"My coaching with Jamie has taught me to do what I have to do without procrastinating. I feel empowered and confident that my decisions are justified and I am better able to follow through without fear. My growing ability to have tough conversations has gotten me to trust myself and stop avoiding them. This has eased my stress significantly. The key to Jamie's coaching has been her consistent focus on these issues in a way I have never been able to do on my own."

—Marilyn Schlossbach
Chef/Restaurateur

"I just reviewed my 2011 financial statements with a business advisor who said, "Wow, 30% growth in a bad economy. Maybe I should be doing what you are!" So, what did I do? I hired Jamie! She helped me see how to step up and be a better leader. I no longer run from hard conversations, ignore troubling situations, repair other people's drama, or fail to follow through. My business now has huge financial growth AND a balanced culture of communication, creativity and learning. In over 100 sessions Jamie and I built a lasting relationship, and I can't imagine my business without her."

—Christine Zilinski
Industry Leader and Owner of Salon Concrete

"I met Jamie shortly after landing my dream job. Although I was experienced, I found myself confronted with conversations that were being spoken in languages that were seemingly foreign to me. I decided to invest my energy and resources into my growth by engaging her services. In every session with Jamie, I come away with more insight, knowledge and skill than before. My stress level has been dramatically decreased in such a short time, due to our work together. Now the pieces of data are locked together creating a framework for me which is the basis of all the important conversations present in my life. Jamie is the glue that holds those pieces together. It is so difficult to quantify the value she has brought to my life and her role in changing the way I see the world each and every day. I will be forever grateful."

—Donna
Healthcare Executive

"My initial goal in coaching was to create a better relationship with my sister (and partner) to build our company. But, thanks to Jamie's expert coaching, I shifted the goal to also include a journey to become a great leader! I learned I need to be visionary as well as pragmatic. Jamie taught me communication and leadership tools that are transforming my leadership every day. I've learned how to delegate and make powerful decisions with meaning, clarity, and strength. Thanks to Jamie's insightful coaching, my biggest realization was that I've read about this stuff for years, but when I'm connected in a coaching moment, the relatedness makes all the pieces connect. This has led me to shift my goal again to becoming a better coach for our team, so they can experience the same growth and success I have."

—Richard Bach
Restaurateur

"I hired Jamie Turner to coach my manager on her leadership and management skills. The results have been astonishing and quantifiable. In just twelve weeks, our average ticket at both centers improved by 10 percent."

—Rob Bixon
CEO, Business Gift Company
European Wax Center Franchisee

"My work stress has been reduced by being able to voice my opinion. I never felt comfortable or even that I had the right to speak up. I used to get defensive about other people's feelings. Now I'm able to look at feedback as a positive thing in my life and in the workplace. Jamie's teachings have spilled over to my life outside of work. I even feel closer to my mom. I used to snap at her and be impatient or not care how she felt."

—Gina Shevick
Hair Colorist, Salon Concrete

"As a result of Jamie's coaching, I have grown in my ability to be able to handle situations with people. I go back to the five words all the time. I constantly use that tool. I've become a person who can clearly let people know how a situation is affecting me and set them up with expectations. I'm not just hoping they read my mind and this has made our team and business soar."

—Connie Alvierto
European Wax Center District Manager

"My coaching experience has been extremely profound. With Jamie's very well-tailored guidance, clear knowledge and experience, as well as her personable, trustworthy, and fun approach, I have been able to discover my strengths and identify areas of improvement, learn how to ask myself the tough questions, and probably for the first time in my life be able to articulate my truth. Jamie not only provides the tools to frame my future goals but also to understand myself and make me the most effective person I can be. She truly cares about my success as much as I do!"

—Lisa Aquino
Owner of Brahma Yoga Spa

Index

About the Author

Jamie Sussel Turner, M.Ed is a business coach, leadership consultant, and author. Her client list includes a wide range of leaders from senior level executives to managers to small business owners. She works with individual leaders and their teams to build a strong foundation of vision, mission, and core values. Sussel Turner also provides ongoing workshops to deepen and strengthen her clients' knowledge and application of leadership and communication skills.

Sussel Turner's coaching is results-oriented, deeply thoughtful, provocative, and proven to reduce her clients' stress by up to 75 percent. This book is the culmination of the strategies and mind-altering thinking that has helped her clients gain access to a new way of being and leading so they can create the businesses and lives of their dreams.

Sussel Turner served in educational leadership positions for twenty years, the last twelve as a school principal. It was in that position that she recognized how the stress of her job was interfering with her ability to help her school community reach their goals.

Her journey to coaching was sparked during a first-time meeting with a neighbor during a New Jersey beach clean-up in 2002. When she asked, "What do you do?" and the neighbor replied, "I'm a coach," the light bulbs started flashing in Sussel Turner's mind with immediate recognition that coaching would be her post-education career shift. This revelation led her to apply for and receive a grant from the Geraldine R. Dodge Foundation to become a certified coach in 2005. She serves on the executive board and professional development committee of ICF-NJ (International Coach Federation of New Jersey).

Sussel Turner retired as a principal in 2009 and mentored and taught future principals at NJ EXCEL (EXpedited Certification for Educational Leadership) while simultaneously launching her coaching business. She became a certified facilitator of Fierce Conversations in 2008 and a certified social + emotional intelligence coach in 2013. She has published a blog since 2011, and she is most proud of having overcome her extreme difficultly as a writer to become an author. She believes it is our struggles in overcoming challenges that lead to the sweetest tasting triumph of all.

Sussel Turner earned dual masters degrees in educational leadership and elementary education, and her leadership approach has been featured in journals and newspaper articles including *The New York Times*.

Made in the USA
Lexington, KY
21 June 2014